Contents

Party snacks 4

Soups 12

Starters 22

Main dishes 42

Desserts 74

Index 96

Salami rolls

Overall timing 45 minutes plus chilling

Freezing Not suitable

Makes 12

1¼ pints	Light stock	700 ml
2 teasp	Wine vinegar	2x5 ml
1 tbsp	Dry sherry	15 ml
	Pinch of sugar	
2 tbsp	Powdered gelatine	2x15 ml
8 oz	Cream cheese	225 g
1 tbsp	Soured cream	15 ml
2 tbsp	Grated Parmesan cheese	2x15 ml
4 oz	Bottle of cocktail onions	110 g
12	Large salami slices	12
	Thick mayonnaise	
	Parsley	

Put the stock, vinegar, sherry and sugar into a saucepan and bring to the boil. Remove from heat and strain through muslin or a very fine sieve. Leave to cool.

Put gelatine and a little of the stock into a heatproof bowl over a saucepan of boiling water. Stir until gelatine has dissolved. Add to the cooled stock. Pour into a greased cake tin and chill in refrigerator till set.

Mix together cream cheese and soured cream. Stir in the Parmesan. Drain and finely chop the onions and stir into the cheese mixture. Put a little of the mixture on to each salami slice. Pull the slice together and secure with half a cocktail stick.

Remove jellied stock from tin and chop it roughly with a dampened knife. Spoon the chopped jelly over a serving dish. Arrange the salami rolls on top. Garnish with thick mayonnaise, chopped parsley and parsley sprigs.

ENTERTAINING AT HOME

Edited by Norma MacMillan and Wendy James
Home economist Gilly Cubitt

ORBIS PUBLISHING London

Introduction

When you are entertaining, you want to produce a rather special meal. We have selected a range of imaginative dishes, some extravagant, some inexpensive, to enable you to impress your family and friends.

Both imperial and metric measures are given for each recipe; you should follow only one set of measures as they are not direct conversions. All spoon measures are level unless otherwise stated. Pastry quantities are based on the amount of flour used. Dried herbs may be substituted for fresh herbs: use one-third of the quantity.

Photographs were supplied by Editions Atlas, Editions Atlas/Cedus, Editions Atlas/Masson, Editions Atlas/Zadora, Archivio IGDA, Lavinia Press Agency, Orbis GmbH, Wales Tourist Board

The material in this book has previously appeared in *The Complete Cook*

First published 1981 in Great Britain by Orbis Publishing Limited, 20–22 Bedfordbury, London WC2

ISBN 0-85613-371-X
Printed in Singapore

Kipper toasts

Overall timing 15 minutes

Freezing Not suitable

Makes 10

6	Kipper fillets	6
1 tbsp	Lemon juice	15 ml
3 oz	Softened butter	75 g
1 tbsp	Made mustard	15 ml
10	Slices of bread	10
1	Large onion	1
1 tbsp	Thick mayonnaise	15 ml
	Parsley	

Place kippers upright in a jug, fill with boiling water and leave for 5 minutes. Drain well, then sprinkle with lemon juice.

Mix butter with mustard. Toast the bread on both sides, then cut off the crusts. Spread mustard butter on toast while still hot. Cut kippers into thin strips to fit toast.

Peel and finely chop onion and mix with mayonnaise. Place a spoonful of onion mixture on each kipper toast. Arrange on serving plate and garnish with parsley sprigs.

Asparagus boats

Overall timing 30 minutes plus chilling

Freezing Not suitable

Makes 12

6 oz	Rich shortcrust pastry	175 g
2x10 oz	Cans of asparagus tips	2x280 g
12 tbsp	Thick mayonnaise	12x15 ml

Preheat the oven to 425°F (220°C) Gas 7.

Roll out dough thinly and use to line 12 barquette (boat-shaped) tins. Prick lightly with a fork. Bake blind for 12–15 minutes. Remove from oven and turn out on to a wire rack to cool.

Drain the asparagus tips on kitchen paper. Spoon or pipe a little mayonnaise into the bottom of each pastry boat. Divide the asparagus tips between the pastry boats, trimming if necessary. Garnish with more mayonnaise.

Mushroom bouchées

Overall timing 40 minutes

Freezing Suitable: reheat cases in oven for 3–5 minutes before filling

Makes about 30

1¼ lb	Frozen puff pastry	600 g
1	Egg	1
Mushroom sauce		
½ pint	Milk	300 ml
	Slice of onion	
	Slice of carrot	
½	Stalk of celery	½
1	Bay leaf	1
4 oz	Button mushrooms	125 g
2 oz	Butter	50 g
2 oz	Plain flour	50 g
½ pint	Light stock	300 ml
4 tbsp	Single cream	4 x 15 ml
	Salt and pepper	

Thaw pastry. Preheat the oven to 425°F (220°C) Gas 7.

Roll out dough to ¼ inch (6mm) thick. Stamp out rounds with a 2 inch (5cm) pastry cutter and arrange in dampened roasting tin. Press 1 inch (2.5cm) cutter into centre of each round, cutting only about halfway through. Beat egg and brush over tops, avoiding outside edges. Place rack upside down over tin to prevent bouchées overturning as they rise. Bake for 15 minutes till crisp and golden. Cut out and discard the pastry middles. Place cases upside down on wire rack and bake for further 2–3 minutes.

Put milk in saucepan with vegetables and bay leaf. Bring to the boil and remove from heat. Cover and infuse for 15 minutes.

Meanwhile, thinly slice mushrooms. Melt butter and fry mushrooms till golden. Stir in flour and cook for 1 minute. Gradually add stock and strained milk. Bring to the boil, stirring, and cook till thickened.

Remove from heat and stir in cream and seasoning. Fill bouchée cases and serve hot.

Ham and chicken puffs

Overall timing 1½ hours

Freezing Not suitable

Makes about 30

3 oz	Fresh breadcrumbs	75 g
	Milk	
4 oz	Cooked chicken meat	125 g
5 oz	Cooked ham	150 g
2 oz	Grated Parmesan cheese	50 g
	Salt and pepper	
4 oz	Choux paste	125 g
	Pinch of powdered mustard	
	Oil for frying	

Soak breadcrumbs in a little milk, then squeeze dry. Mince chicken and ham and mix with the Parmesan and breadcrumbs. Add seasoning to taste and mix well. Shape into about 30 small balls.

Make choux paste, adding mustard with the flour.

Heat oil in deep-fryer to 350°F (180°C). Using two teaspoons, coat chicken balls with choux paste and drop into hot oil. Fry for 5–10 minutes till golden. Remove from pan with a draining spoon and drain well on kitchen paper. Keep hot till all the choux balls have been fried. Arrange on warmed serving dish and serve immediately with tomato or tartare sauce.

Almond-coated cheesies

Overall timing 1 hour 5 minutes

Freezing Not suitable

Makes about 35

7 oz	Plain flour	200 g
5 oz	Mature Cheddar cheese	150 g
9 fl oz	Water	250 ml
3 oz	Butter	75 g
	Salt	
4	Eggs	4
	Oil for frying	
6 oz	Flaked almonds	175 g

Sift flour. Grate cheese. Put water, butter and a pinch of salt in a saucepan and heat gently till butter has melted. Bring to the boil and add sifted flour all at once. Beat vigorously with a wooden spoon until smooth and paste leaves the sides of the pan clean. Remove from heat and cool slightly, then add eggs one at a time. Beat in cheese.

Heat oil in deep-fryer to 350°F (180°C). Place almonds in a shallow dish. With lightly oiled hands, form walnut-sized balls from the choux paste, then roll them in the almonds till well coated.

Fry in the hot oil, in batches, for about 5 minutes, till golden. Lift out with draining spoon and drain on kitchen paper. Serve hot and provide cocktail sticks to pick them up.

Liver and mushroom bites

Overall timing 40 minutes

Freezing Not suitable

Makes 32

8 oz	Button mushrooms	225 g
8 oz	Lamb's liver	225 g
4 oz	Smoked back bacon	125 g
2 oz	Butter	50 g
	Salt and pepper	
8	Small slices of bread	8

Thinly slice the mushrooms. Slice the liver. Derind and chop the bacon. Melt half the butter in a saucepan, add bacon and fry till light brown. Add the mushrooms and cook for a further 5 minutes.

Melt the remaining butter in a frying pan, add the liver and fry over a high heat for 5 minutes, stirring frequently. Season and remove from heat. Allow to cool slightly, then purée in a blender.

Add bacon and mushrooms to liver with seasoning and mix well. Toast the bread, removing crusts if liked, and spread with the hot paste. Cut each slice into quarters. Garnish with parsley and serve immediately.

Caraway twists

Overall timing 30 minutes

Freezing Not suitable

Makes about 40

7½ oz	Frozen puff pastry	212 g
2	Egg yolks	2
½ teasp	Salt	2.5 ml
2 tbsp	Caraway seeds	2 x 15 ml

Thaw pastry. Preheat oven to 425°F (220°C) Gas. 7.

Roll out dough on floured surface to ¼ inch (6 mm) thickness and 10 inch (25 cm) square. Cut square into strips ½ inch (12.5 mm) wide, then cut these in half making sticks 5 inches (13 cm) long.

Beat egg yolks with salt. Brush over the dough sticks and sprinkle with caraway seeds. Using a spatula, lift sticks on to greased baking trays, twisting some (hold stick at both ends and turn in opposite directions). Bake for 10 minutes. Cool on a wire rack.

Hot stuffed olives

Overall timing 50 minutes plus cooling

Freezing Not suitable

Serves 8–10

4 oz	Salami	125 g
4 oz	Lean veal	125 g
1 oz	Butter	25 g
5 tbsp	White wine	5x15 ml
¼ pint	Light stock	150 ml
4 oz	Fresh breadcrumbs	125 g
1 tbsp	Chopped parsley	15 ml
¼ teasp	Grated nutmeg	1.25 ml
2	Eggs	2
	Salt and pepper	
12 oz	Large green olives	350 g
3 tbsp	Plain flour	3x15 ml
8 tbsp	Oil	8x15 ml

Remove rind from salami and push twice through mincer with veal, till very finely minced. Melt butter in a saucepan and fry meats for 10 minutes, stirring frequently. Add wine and stock and cook for 10 minutes.

Stir half breadcrumbs into mixture with parsley, nutmeg, one egg and seasoning. Cool.

Meanwhile, stone olives using an olive stoner. Put stuffing into a piping bag fitted with a small plain nozzle. Hold an olive with one finger over one end of the hole. Insert nozzle into other end and squeeze bag gently, withdrawing it slowly as olive is filled. Make any remaining stuffing into olive-sized balls.

Beat remaining egg. Toss stuffed olives (and stuffing balls) in flour, then dip into beaten egg and coat with remaining breadcrumbs. Heat remaining oil in a frying pan and fry olives (and stuffing balls) for about 5 minutes till crisp and golden. Drain on kitchen paper and serve hot.

Savoury stuffed prunes

Overall timing 50 minutes plus soaking

Freezing Not suitable

Makes 16

16	Large plump prunes	16
4 oz	Cottage cheese	125 g
2 teasp	Milk	2x5 ml
	Grated rind of ½ orange	
1 oz	Roasted salted peanuts	25 g
	Salt and pepper	

Put the prunes into a bowl, cover with warm water and soak for 1 hour. Tip the prunes and soaking liquid into a saucepan, cover and simmer for 10 minutes till tender. Drain and leave to cool.

Cut the prunes across lengthways and carefully remove stones.

Press the cottage cheese through a sieve into a bowl. Beat in the milk and orange rind. Finely chop the peanuts and add half to the cheese with seasoning. Mix well. Pipe or spoon the mixture into the prunes so the stuffing shows slightly. Sprinkle with the remaining peanuts. Arrange on lettuce leaves in serving dish.

Consommé

Overall timing 6 hours

Freezing Suitable: add sherry after reheating

To serve 6

1 lb	Marrow bone, sawn into pieces	450 g
1	Knuckle of veal	1
1 lb	Shin of beef	450 g
2	Onions	2
2	Carrots	2
1	Stalk of celery	1
	Bouquet garni	
6	Black peppercorns	6
3½ pints	Water	1.7 litres
8 oz	Lean stewing beef	225 g
1	Egg white	1
2 tbsp	Dry sherry	2x15 ml
	Salt	

Preheat the oven to 425°F (220°C) Gas 7.

Put marrow bone, veal knuckle and shin of beef in a roasting tin. Bake for about 30 minutes, turning occasionally, till browned. Transfer to a large saucepan.

Add onions, carrots and celery to the pan with bouquet garni, peppercorns and water and bring to the boil. Skim off any scum, cover and simmer for 3 hours. Strain and leave to cool.

Mince the stewing beef into a large saucepan and add the cold stock and egg white. Heat gently, whisking, till egg white forms a thick froth on the soup. Stop whisking and bring slowly to just below boiling point. Reduce heat to a gentle simmer so the foam is not disturbed. Simmer for 1½ hours.

Pour soup carefully into a scalded jelly bag, letting the foam fall gently into the bag after the soup has run through. Pour the soup through again – it should be very clear and glossy.

Add sherry and salt to taste. Either reheat gently and serve hot, or chill and spoon the jellied consommé into chilled bowls to serve.

Chicory soup

Overall timing 25 minutes

Freezing Suitable: add vermouth after reheating

To serve 4

4	Heads of chicory	4
2½ oz	Butter	65 g
2 teasp	Caster sugar	2x5 ml
1¾ pints	Chicken stock	1 litre
2 teasp	Plain flour	2x5 ml
3 fl oz	Dry vermouth	90 ml
	Salt and pepper	

Chop chicory. Melt 2 oz (50 g) of the butter in a saucepan and fry chicory over a gentle heat for about 5 minutes. Tilt pan, add sugar and allow to caramelize. Add stock, cover and simmer for 10 minutes.

Mix remaining butter with the flour to a smooth paste. Stir paste a little at a time into the soup. Return to the boil and simmer for 2–3 minutes.

Add vermouth and seasoning and cook, uncovered, for 1–2 minutes more. Pour into serving bowls and garnish with freshly made, hot croûtons.

Onion soup with wine

Overall timing 45 minutes

Freezing Suitable: pour soup over bread and add cheese after reheating

To serve 4

3	Large onions	3
2 oz	Butter	50 g
1 tbsp	Plain flour	15 ml
½ teasp	Brown sugar	2.5 ml
2½ pints	Water	1.5 litres
8	Slices of French bread	8
2 tbsp	Dry white wine	2x15 ml
	Salt and pepper	
2 oz	Gruyère or Cheddar cheese	50 g

Peel and slice onions. Melt half the butter in a large saucepan and cook onions till transparent. Sprinkle onions with flour. Cook, stirring, until flour colours. Add sugar, then gradually stir in water. Simmer for 20 minutes.

Preheat the oven to 450°F (230°C) Gas 8.

Fry bread in remaining butter. Place bread slices in bottom of individual bowls or ovenproof soup tureen. Add wine and seasoning, then pour soup over bread. Grate cheese and sprinkle it into the bowls. Bake for 5–10 minutes to melt the cheese.

Prawn soup

Overall timing 50 minutes

Freezing Not suitable

To serve 4

½	Onion	½
1	Stalk of celery	1
1 lb	Large prawns	450 g
2 pints	Chicken or fish stock	1.1 litres
1	Bay leaf	1
	Salt and pepper	
3 oz	Butter	75 g
2	Eggs	2
2 tbsp	Fresh breadcrumbs	2x15 ml
	Grated nutmeg	
¼ teasp	Crushed fennel seeds	1.25 ml
1 tbsp	Chopped parsley	15 ml
2 tbsp	Plain flour	2x15 ml
1 tbsp	Lemon juice	15 ml
5 tbsp	Single cream	5x15 ml

Peel and chop onion; trim and chop celery. Remove heads and legs from prawns and add to stock with onion, celery, bay leaf and seasoning. Bring to the boil, cover and simmer for 15 minutes.

Meanwhile, carefully remove prawns from their shells, keeping shells intact. Chop prawns.

Melt 1 oz (25 g) of the butter in a saucepan. Beat eggs till frothy, add to pan and stir over a gentle heat till lightly scrambled. Add to prawns. Stir in breadcrumbs, nutmeg, fennel, parsley and seasoning. Stuff the mixture into the prawn shells, packing it in firmly.

Strain stock. Melt remaining butter in a saucepan, stir in flour and cook for 1 minute. Gradually add stock and lemon juice and bring to the boil, stirring till thickened. Add stuffed prawn shells and simmer for 2 minutes. Remove from heat and stir in cream.

Lift prawn shells out of soup, divide between soup bowls and ladle soup over.

Chestnut and rice soup

Overall timing 1¼ hours

Freezing Suitable

To serve 4

1 lb	Fresh chestnuts	450 g
¾ pint	Boiling water	400 ml
¾ pint	Stock	400 ml
	Salt	
3 oz	Long grain rice	75 g
1 pint	Milk	560 ml
1 oz	Butter	25 g
	Ground cinnamon	

Make slits round chestnuts from base to point. Cook in boiling water for 5 minutes. Drain, then shell and skin. Place chestnuts in a saucepan with stock, add salt and bring to boil. Cook for 20 minutes.

Remove half the chestnuts and sieve or purée in a blender; put on one side. Add the rice to the remaining chestnuts and simmer for 10 minutes.

Stir in the chestnut purée, milk and butter and cook gently for a further 10 minutes, stirring occasionally to prevent soup from sticking. Add salt and a pinch of cinnamon to taste. Serve very hot.

Normandy chicken soup

Overall timing 50 minutes

Freezing Suitable: add egg yolk and cream after reheating

To serve 6

8 oz	Chicken breast	225 g
	Bay leaf	
1¾ pints	Milk	1 litre
6 tbsp	Calvados or brandy	6x15 ml
8 oz	Button mushrooms	225 g
2 oz	Butter	50 g
4 tbsp	Plain flour	4x15 ml
1 tbsp	Lemon juice	15 ml
¼ teasp	Grated nutmeg	1.25 ml
1 tbsp	Chopped parsley	15 ml
	Salt and pepper	
1	Egg yolk	1
4 tbsp	Single cream	4x15 ml

Put chicken breast in a saucepan with bay leaf and milk and bring to the boil. Cover and simmer for about 15 minutes till tender. Remove chicken from milk. Discard any bones and skin and cut meat into strips. Put into a shallow bowl and pour Calvados or brandy over. Marinate for 20 minutes.

Meanwhile, thickly slice mushrooms. Melt butter in a large saucepan, add mushrooms and fry gently for 5 minutes without browning. Stir in flour and cook for 1 minute. Gradually add strained milk and bring to the boil, stirring. Add lemon juice and nutmeg and simmer for 5 minutes.

Add chicken and marinade with parsley and seasoning. Simmer for a further 5 minutes.

Lightly beat egg yolk and cream in a bowl. Pour in a little of the soup, stirring constantly. Pour back into the soup and cook, stirring, for 3 minutes; do not boil. Serve hot.

Manhattan clam chowder

Overall timing 2 hours

Freezing Suitable

To serve 8

4 oz	Streaky bacon	125 g
2 tbsp	Oil	2x15 ml
3	Large onions	3
2	Large tomatoes	2
2	Leeks	2
1	Stalk of celery	1
1	Carrot	1
2	Potatoes	2
1½ pints	Fish stock	850 ml
2	Sprigs of parsley	2
1	Bay leaf	1
¼ teasp	Grated nutmeg	1.25 ml
	Salt and pepper	
¾ pint	Milk	400 ml
1 lb	Canned clams	450 g
1 oz	Butter	25 g
1 oz	Plain flour	25 g
2 teasp	Worcestershire sauce	2x5 ml
¼ teasp	Tabasco sauce	1.25 ml

Derind and dice bacon. Heat oil in a saucepan, add bacon and cook gently. Peel and slice onions and add to pan. Cook till transparent.

Blanch and peel tomatoes. Finely chop leeks and celery. Peel and finely chop carrot and potatoes. Add to pan and cook for 2–3 minutes. Add stock, parsley, bay leaf, nutmeg and seasoning. Cover and simmer for 10 minutes.

Discard parsley and bay leaf. Purée soup in blender, return to rinsed-out pan and add milk and drained clams. Simmer gently for 4 minutes.

Knead butter and flour to a paste. Stir into soup in tiny pieces. Cook for 2–3 minutes until thick. Stir in Worcestershire and Tabasco sauces and serve.

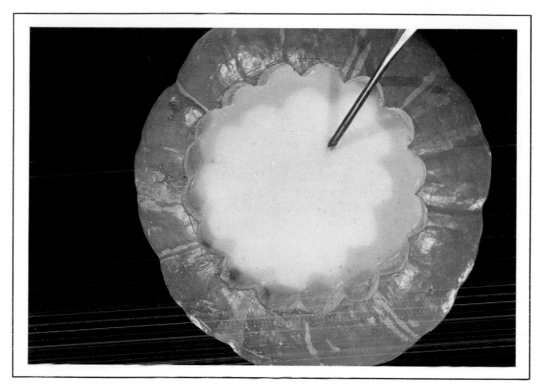

Pumpkin soup

Overall timing 50 minutes

Freezing Not suitable

To serve 6

2 lb	Pumpkin or other squash	900 g
½ pint	Water	300 ml
	Salt and pepper	
1½ pints	Milk	850 ml
1 teasp	Sugar	5 ml
¼ teasp	Grated nutmeg	1.25 ml
1	Egg yolk	1
4 tbsp	Single cream	4 x 15 ml

Prepare the squash, discarding fibrous centre and seeds. Cut the flesh into chunks, put into a saucepan with the water and salt and bring to the boil. Simmer for about 30 minutes till tender, then purée in a blender or food mill. Place purée in saucepan with milk, sugar and nutmeg. Heat through gently till almost boiling, stirring occasionally.

Beat the egg yolk and cream together in a bowl and pour in a little of the hot soup, stirring constantly. Pour back into the pan and stir over a low heat for 3 minutes – do not boil. Taste and adjust seasoning, then serve immediately with toasted rye bread.

Chilled cucumber and mint soup

Overall timing 10 minutes plus maceration

Freezing Not suitable

To serve 4

1	Large cucumber	1
½ pint	Milk	300 ml
1	Garlic clove	1
1½ pints	Natural yogurt	850 ml
	Salt and pepper	
12	Fresh mint leaves	12

Peel the cucumber with a potato peeler, then cut in two. Slice one half lengthways into four and cut each quarter into thin slices. Put slices in a bowl. Chop remaining half and place in blender with milk. Blend till smooth.

Peel and crush the garlic and put into blender with the yogurt and seasoning. Blend for 2 seconds, then pour over the sliced cucumber.

Wash, dry and roughly chop mint leaves. Sprinkle over the cucumber and yogurt mixture. Leave to macerate in the refrigerator for 2 hours.

Stir in the mint and taste and adjust the seasoning. Serve immediately with breadsticks.

Watercress soup

Overall timing 40 minutes

Freezing Suitable: add cream after thawing

To serve 4

1	Large onion	1
2	Large floury potatoes	2
1 oz	Butter	25 g
3	Bunches of watercress	3
1¾ pints	Chicken stock	1 litre
	Salt and pepper	
4 fl oz	Double cream	113 ml

Peel and finely chop onion. Peel and chop or grate potatoes. Melt butter in a saucepan, add onions and potatoes and turn till coated in butter. Cover and cook gently for 10 minutes.

Wash, dry and chop watercress leaves and stalks, reserving some whole leaves. Add to pan with stock and bring to boil. Cover and simmer for 15 minutes.

Rub soup through sieve or purée in blender. Return to pan, add reserved watercress leaves and reheat. Taste and adjust seasoning. Serve immediately with side dish of whipped cream, or cool, stir in cream and chill well before serving.

Fish goujonettes

Overall timing 20 minutes

Freezing Suitable: reheat in 375°F (190°C) Gas 5 oven for 30 minutes

To serve 8

	Oil for frying	
2 lb	Mixed white fish fillets	900 g
¼ pint	Milk	150 ml
	Salt and pepper	
3 oz	Plain flour	75 g
	Sprigs of parsley	
2	Lemons	2

Heat oil in a deep-fryer to 340°F (170°C).

Skin fish and cut into thin strips. Dip into milk, then coat in seasoned flour.

Fry the strips of fish in the oil till golden brown. Remove from pan with a draining spoon and drain on kitchen paper. Garnish with sprigs of parsley and lemon wedges and serve with tartare sauce.

Moules à la marinière

Overall timing 30 minutes

Freezing Not suitable

To serve 6

4 pints	Mussels	2.2 litres
1	Onion	1
1	Leek	1
2	Garlic cloves	2
2 oz	Butter	50 g
½ pint	Dry white wine	300 ml
1 tbsp	Plain flour	15 ml
	Salt and pepper	
1 tbsp	Chopped parsley	15 ml

Scrub mussels. Peel and chop the onion. Trim and chop the leek. Peel and crush garlic. Melt half the butter in a deep, heavy-based saucepan and fry the onion, garlic and leek for 5 minutes.

Add the wine and bring to the boil. Add the mussels and cook for a few minutes till the shells open, shaking the pan from time to time. Discard any unopened mussels.

Place the open mussels in a heatproof serving dish over a pan of boiling water to keep hot. Pour the cooking liquor through a muslin-lined sieve and return to the pan. Boil over a high heat till reduced by a third.

Mix the remaining butter and flour together to make a paste. Add in small pieces to the cooking liquor, stirring constantly. Bring to the boil, season and cook, stirring, for 5 minutes.

Sprinkle chopped parsley over mussels. Pour the sauce over, cover and leave for a few minutes for flavours to be absorbed. Serve hot with fresh crusty bread, and provide soup spoons.

Ham and spinach hors d'oeuvre

Overall timing 35 minutes plus thawing and cooling

Freezing Not suitable

To serve 4

7 oz	Frozen puff pastry	212 g
12 oz	Frozen spinach	350 g
	Salt and pepper	
4	Slices of smoked ham	4
1 oz	Butter	25 g
2 tbsp	Chopped onion	2x15 ml
$\frac{1}{4}$ pint	White sauce	150 ml
1	Egg yolk	1
2 oz	Cheese	50 g
2 tbsp	Single cream	2x15 ml

Thaw pastry and spinach. Preheat the oven to 425°F (220°C) Gas 7.

Roll out dough to $\frac{1}{4}$ inch (6 mm) thickness. Using $3\frac{1}{2}$ inch (9 cm) pastry cutter, cut four rounds. Place them upside down on greased baking tray. Bake for 10–15 minutes till well risen and golden. Cool.

Meanwhile, chop spinach and place in a sieve to drain. Season with salt and pepper. Using pastry cutter, cut four rounds out of the ham; finely chop the trimmings.

Melt butter in a saucepan and cook onion till golden brown. Add chopped ham, half the white sauce and seasoning and stir well. Divide half the mixture between pastry rounds, cover with ham rounds, then top with the spinach. Place in ovenproof dish.

Stir egg yolk, grated cheese and cream into remaining sauce and pour over spinach. Bake for 10 minutes till cheese is golden brown and bubbling. Serve immediately.

Fish Bengali

Overall timing 1 hour

Freezing Not suitable

To serve 6

9	Sole or other white fish fillets	9
¾ pint	Water	400 ml
1	Bay leaf	1
6	Black peppercorns	6
1	Garlic clove	1
1	Small onion	1
3	Medium-size tomatoes	3
	Ground cinnamon	
	Salt and pepper	
2	Eggs	2
4 oz	Fresh breadcrumbs	125 g
2 oz	Butter	50 g
3 tbsp	Oil	3 x 15 ml

Remove skin from three fish fillets. Put skinned fillets into a frying pan, add water, bay leaf and peppercorns and bring to the boil. Cover and simmer till tender.

Remove fish from pan and flake into a bowl. Peel and crush garlic. Peel and finely chop onion. Blanch, peel and chop tomatoes. Add all to bowl with a pinch of cinnamon and seasoning. Mash together with a fork.

Arrange remaining fish fillets, skin side up, on a board. Spread mashed fish over, roll up and secure with wooden cocktail sticks. Lightly beat eggs with a pinch of salt. Brush over fish rolls, then coat with breadcrumbs.

Heat butter and oil in frying pan, add fish rolls and fry for 15 minutes, turning frequently, till tender and golden all over. Drain on kitchen paper, remove cocktail sticks and arrange fish on warmed serving dish. Garnish with lettuce and sliced tomatoes and serve with lemon wedges.

Anchovy ramekins

Overall timing 45 minutes

Freezing Not suitable

To serve 6

2 lb	Cooked potatoes	900 g
2½ oz	Butter	65 g
	A little hot milk	
2	Cans of anchovy fillets	2
	Pepper	
3 tbsp	Breadcrumbs	3x15 ml
3 tbsp	Grated Parmesan cheese	3x15 ml

Preheat the oven to 375°F (190°C) Gas 5.

Sieve or mash potatoes well. Beat in 2 oz (50 g) butter and enough hot milk to give a smooth creamy consistency.

Drain anchovies. Set aside four and finely chop the rest. Stir them into potatoes with black pepper to taste. Divide mixture between six lightly-buttered ramekin dishes.

Mix together breadcrumbs and cheese and sprinkle over potato mixture. Top with reserved anchovies, chopped. Dot with remaining butter and place ramekins on a baking tray. Bake for 15–20 minutes.

Stuffed mushrooms

Overall timing 50 minutes

Freezing Not suitable

To serve 4–6

16	Medium-size cup mushrooms	16
4	Large tomatoes	4
1	Onion	1
1	Garlic clove	1
3 tbsp	Olive oil	3x15 ml
1 oz	Fresh breadcrumbs	25 g
1 tbsp	Chopped parsley	15 ml
	Salt and pepper	
4 teasp	Dried breadcrumbs	4x5 ml

Preheat the oven to 400°F (200°C) Gas 6.

Separate mushroom stalks from the caps. Finely chop stalks. Blanch, peel and chop the tomatoes. Peel and finely chop onion. Peel and crush garlic.

Heat 2 tbsp (2x15 ml) of the oil in a frying pan and fry the onion for 5 minutes. Add the mushroom stalks and tomatoes and cook for a further 5 minutes, stirring occasionally. Add garlic, fresh breadcrumbs, chopped parsley and seasoning. Mix well and remove from the heat.

Arrange the mushroom caps in greased ovenproof dish. Season lightly, then divide the stuffing between the mushroom caps. Trickle the remaining oil over and sprinkle with the dried breadcrumbs. Bake for 20 minutes. Arrange on a warmed serving dish and serve immediately.

Individual cauliflower cheeses

Overall timing 35 minutes

Freezing Not suitable

To serve 6

1	Small cauliflower	1
	Salt and pepper	
15 oz	Can of artichoke hearts	425 g
1 oz	Butter	25 g
Cheese sauce		
1 oz	Butter	25 g
1 oz	Plain flour	25 g
½ pint	Milk	300 ml
4 oz	Gruyère or Cheddar cheese	125 g

Preheat the oven to 425°F (220°C) Gas 7.

Divide cauliflower into small florets. Cut away any large stalks. Cook in boiling salted water for about 10 minutes or till tender. Drain.

Drain the artichoke hearts. Put in another saucepan with the butter and heat through gently.

To make the sauce, melt butter in a saucepan. Stir in the flour and cook for 1 minute. Gradually add the milk. Bring to the boil, stirring. Cook gently for 3–4 minutes. Remove from heat and add pepper. Grate cheese and add half of it to the sauce.

Put the artichoke hearts in a greased ovenproof dish. Top each with a cauliflower floret. Pour over the sauce. Sprinkle on remaining cheese. Bake for about 10 minutes until the cheese has melted.

Fish pudding

Overall timing 1½ hours

Freezing Not suitable

To serve 6–8

2 lb	Haddock fillets	900 g
2 tbsp	Plain flour	2 x 15 ml
	Salt and pepper	
2 oz	Softened butter	50 g
¼ pint	Carton of double cream	150 ml
½ pint	Milk	300 ml
1 lb	Whole prawns	450 g
	Sprigs of parsley	
	Lemon wedges and slices	
1 pint	Mushroom sauce (see page 7)	560 ml

Preheat the oven to 400°F (200°C) Gas 6.

Remove skin from fish. Put fish through mincer three times, into a bowl. Add flour and seasoning and pound with a wooden spoon till smooth. Beat in butter, then gradually beat in cream and milk. Spoon into greased 2 pint (1.1 litre) ovenproof dish and smooth the top. Cover with foil and place in a roasting tin containing 1 inch (2.5 cm) hot water. Bake for 1 hour.

Run a knife round the edge of the pudding and turn out on to a warmed serving dish. Shell half the prawns and garnish the pudding with shelled and whole prawns, sprigs of parsley and lemon wedges and slices. Serve immediately with the hot mushroom sauce.

Grapefruit with crab

Overall timing 30 minutes plus chilling

Freezing Not suitable

To serve 4

2 oz	Long grain rice	50 g
	Salt and pepper	
2	Large grapefruit	2
2 oz	Black olives	50 g
6 oz	Can of crab meat	170 g
¼ pint	Thick mayonnaise	150 ml

Cook the rice in boiling salted water for 15–20 minutes till tender. Cool under running water and drain well.

Cut grapefruit in half. Remove flesh with a grapefruit knife, chop and put into a bowl. Retain shells.

Stone olives. Reserve a few whole ones for the garnish and slice the rest. Add to the bowl with the rice and drained and flaked crab meat. Mix in two-thirds of the mayonnaise and seasoning.

Fill grapefruit shells with the crab mixture. Decorate with remaining mayonnaise and reserved whole olives. Chill before serving.

Camembert and pickle salad

Overall timing 15 minutes plus chilling

Freezing Not suitable

To serve 4

5 oz	Camembert cheese	150 g
1	Small onion	1
9½ fl oz	Bottle of mixed pickles	269 ml
½	Red pepper	½
	Sprigs of parsley	
Dressing		
1 tbsp	Lemon juice	15 ml
¼ teasp	Caster sugar	1.25 ml
¼ teasp	Salt	1.25 ml
	Chilli sauce	
4 tbsp	Oil	4x15 ml

Cut Camembert into small cubes. Peel onion and cut into rings. Drain pickles, reserving 1 tbsp (15 ml) of the vinegar. Chop any large pieces of pickled vegetable. Deseed and chop pepper. Mix all together in salad bowl.

To make dressing, beat together the reserved vinegar, lemon juice, sugar, salt, a few drops of chilli sauce and the oil. Taste and adjust seasoning. Pour over salad and lightly mix in. Chill for 30 minutes. Serve garnished with parsley.

Spicy avocado mousse

Overall timing 15 minutes plus 3 hours chilling

Freezing Not suitable

To serve 4

2 teasp	Powdered gelatine	2x5 ml
2	Large ripe avocados	2
2 tbsp	Lemon juice	2x15 ml
	Salt	
	Tabasco sauce	
2 tbsp	Brined green peppercorns	2x15 ml
¼ pint	Carton of double cream	150 ml
4	Lettuce leaves	4
2	Tomatoes	2

Put 4 tbsp (4x15 ml) water into a small heat-proof bowl, sprinkle the gelatine over and leave till spongy. Stand the bowl in a pan of hot water and stir till dissolved. Cool slightly.

Cut the avocados in half lengthways, discard the stones and scoop out the flesh. Put into a blender with the gelatine, lemon juice, salt and three drops of Tabasco. Crush two-thirds of the drained peppercorns with the back of a spoon and add to the blender. Blend to a smooth purée. Pour into a large bowl and chill till syrupy and beginning to set.

Whip the cream till it stands in soft peaks. Fold into the avocado purée with a metal spoon. Pour the mousse into four dampened dishes or moulds and chill till set. Serve garnished with remaining peppercorns, lettuce and tomatoes.

Prawn cocktail

Overall timing 15 minutes plus chilling

Freezing Not suitable

To serve 4

12 oz	Shelled prawns	350 g
	Salt and pepper	
1 tbsp	Lemon juice	15 ml
¼ pint	Thick mayonnaise	150 ml
2 tbsp	Tomato ketchup	2x15 ml
½ teasp	Worcestershire sauce	2.5 ml
2	Lettuce hearts	2
1 teasp	Chopped parsley	5 ml
4	Lemon slices	4
4	Whole prawns	4

Put the shelled prawns into a bowl with seasoning and lemon juice. Chill for 30 minutes.

Mix together the mayonnaise, tomato ketchup, Worcestershire sauce and seasoning.

Wash the lettuce hearts, separate into leaves and dry thoroughly. Use to line four glasses. Arrange the chilled prawns on top of the lettuce and spoon the cocktail sauce over. Sprinkle with parsley.

Make a cut to the centre of each slice of lemon and place on the side of each glass with an unpeeled prawn. Serve immediately with brown bread and butter.

Smoked salmon mornay

Overall timing 45 minutes

Freezing Not suitable

To serve 6

2 oz	Butter	50 g
3 tbsp	Plain flour	3x15 ml
¾ pint	Milk	400 ml
6 oz	Cheese	175 g
	Salt and pepper	
6	Canned artichoke hearts	6
12 oz	Smoked salmon pieces	350 g
1	Lemon	1
	Sprigs of parsley	

Preheat the oven to 425°F (220°C) Gas 7.

Melt the butter in a saucepan, add flour and cook for 1 minute. Gradually add milk and bring to the boil, stirring till thickened. Grate cheese and stir into sauce with seasoning.

Arrange six scallop shells or small oven-proof dishes on a baking tray and place an artichoke heart in each. Spoon half the sauce over. Divide the salmon between the shells to cover the sauce completely. Spoon remaining sauce over salmon. Bake for 15 minutes till the sauce is golden.

Arrange on a serving dish and garnish with the lemon and parsley.

Scallop boats

Overall timing 45 minutes

Freezing Not suitable

To serve 4

13 oz	Frozen puff pastry	375 g
8	Prepared scallops	8
2 tbsp	Plain flour	2x15 ml
1	Small onion	1
3 oz	Butter	75 g
1 tbsp	Chopped parsley	15 ml
	Salt and pepper	
1 tbsp	Fresh breadcrumbs	15 ml
1 tbsp	Grated Parmesan cheese	15 ml

Thaw the pastry. Preheat the oven to 425°F (220°C) Gas 7.

Roll out dough and use to line four scallop shells. Prick and knock up the edges. Press four scallop shells on top and bake for 10 minutes.

Meanwhile, cut scallops in half and toss in flour. Peel and finely chop onion. Melt butter in a saucepan. Add scallops, onion, parsley and seasoning. Cover and cook gently for 10 minutes.

Remove top shells from pastry: bake for 5 more minutes. Remove pastry cases from shells and arrange on baking tray. Divide scallop mixture between cases. Mix breadcrumbs and cheese and sprinkle over top. Bake for a further 5 minutes.

Macaroni nests

Overall timing 50 minutes

Freezing Not suitable

To serve 4

4 oz	Long macaroni	125 g
	Salt and pepper	
4 oz	Cooked ham	125 g
4	Eggs	4
4 teasp	Grated cheese	4x5 ml
1 tbsp	Chopped parsley	15 ml
2	Tomatoes	2
1	Lettuce leaf	1

Preheat the oven to 425°F (220°C) Gas 7.

Cook the macaroni in boiling salted water till tender. Drain in a colander and rinse with cold water.

Starting in the centre of the bottom, line the bottom and sides of four greased ramekins with macaroni. Dice the ham and divide between the ramekins. Break an egg into the centre of each ramekin and season well. Sprinkle with grated cheese and parsley.

Cover ramekins with foil and place in roasting tin with 1 inch (2.5 cm) hot water. Bake for 20 minutes.

Turn out on to a warmed serving plate and garnish with tomato lilies and small pieces of lettuce. Serve with more grated cheese or tomato sauce.

Haitiian avocados

Overall timing 15 minutes

Freezing Not suitable

To serve 4

2	Avocados	2
3 tbsp	Lemon juice	3x15 ml
1 teasp	Worcestershire sauce	5 ml
	Tabasco sauce	
6 oz	Shelled prawns	175 g
4	Lettuce leaves	4
4 tbsp	Thick mayonnaise	4x15 ml

Cut avocados in half lengthways and take out the stones. Remove avocado flesh and dice it. Reserve shells. Place diced flesh in a bowl with the lemon juice, Worcestershire sauce, a few drops of Tabasco and the prawns. Mix till well combined.

Fill avocado shells with the mixture. Chill, then arrange avocados on lettuce leaves. Pipe mayonnaise round the edge of each shell.

Onion tarts

Overall timing 40 minutes

Freezing Suitable: reheat from frozen in 425°F (220°C) Gas 7 oven for 10 minutes

Makes 8

7 oz	Frozen puff pastry	212 g
12 oz	Onions	350 g
4 oz	Smoked bacon	125 g
2 oz	Butter	50 g
3	Eggs	3
½ pint	Milk	300 ml
	Salt and pepper	

Thaw the pastry. Preheat the oven to 425°F (220°C) Gas 7.

Peel and thinly slice the onions. Derind and dice the bacon. Melt the butter in a saucepan and fry the bacon and onions till lightly browned. Cover and sweat for 15 minutes.

Roll out the dough on a lightly floured surface. Stamp out eight rounds with a pastry cutter and use to line eight greased 2½ inch (6.5 cm) tartlet moulds. Prick the bottom of each several times with a fork.

Beat the eggs, milk, onions and bacon. Season and divide between pastry cases. Bake for 10–15 minutes till lightly set and golden.

Garnish with fried onion rings if liked, arrange on a plate with lettuce leaves and serve hot.

French pork spread

Overall timing 4 hours plus setting

Freezing Not suitable

Makes 2½ lb (1.1 kg)

2 lb	Belly of pork rashers	900 g
4 oz	Lard	125 g
1	Garlic clove	1
	Salt and pepper	
¼ teasp	Ground allspice	1.25 ml
½ teasp	Grated nutmeg	2.5 ml
¼ pint	Light stock	150 ml

Preheat the oven to 300°F (150°C) Gas 2.

Trim the pork, discarding any bones, and cut into pieces. Melt the lard in a flameproof casserole and add the pork and peeled garlic clove. Cook gently, stirring, for 15 minutes.

Add 4 teasp (4x5 ml) salt, pepper to taste, the spices and stock. Cover and cook in the oven for 3 hours till the pork is very tender.

Pour off the fat through a fine sieve lined with kitchen paper and reserve if making paste. Discard the garlic clove and serve the pork hot. Alternatively, leave the pork to cool, then mince twice to make a paste. Taste and adjust the seasoning. Pack into sterilized jars and pour the strained fat over. Leave to set so that fat seals the meat. Cover jars securely with the lids.

Country-style liver pâté

Overall timing 3 hours plus maturing

Freezing Suitable

To serve 12

1½ lb	Pig's liver	700 g
1 lb	Back bacon	450 g
8 oz	Lard	225 g
1	Egg	1
1 tbsp	Plain flour	15 ml
	Salt and pepper	
½ teasp	Ground allspice	2.5 ml
1	Pig's caul (optional)	1

Preheat the oven to 350°F (180°C) Gas 4.

Chop the liver. Derind and dice bacon. Put liver and bacon through a fine mincer. Melt the lard in a saucepan and gradually beat into minced liver and bacon in bowl. Beat egg and add with flour, seasoning and allspice. Mix well.

Line greased ovenproof dish with caul, if using, leaving edges hanging over sides. Add liver mixture and smooth top. Wrap caul edges over. Cover dish with lid or foil and place in a roasting tin containing 1 inch (2.5 cm) water. Bake for 1¾ hours.

Allow to cool, then leave in the refrigerator for 2–3 days to mature. Serve with crusty bread.

Hot pâté parcels

Overall timing 45 minutes

Freezing Not suitable

To serve 4

2 oz	Fresh breadcrumbs	50 g
2 tbsp	Milk	2x15 ml
4 oz	Streaky bacon	125 g
2	Onions	2
1 oz	Butter	25 g
12 oz	Minced pork or veal	350 g
2 teasp	Dried mixed herbs	2x5 ml
1	Egg	1
1 tbsp	Brandy (optional)	15 ml
	Salt and pepper	

Preheat the oven to 425°F (220°C) Gas 7.

Soak the breadcrumbs in the milk. Derind and dice bacon. Peel and chop onions. Melt the butter in a frying pan and cook the onions for about 5 minutes or until they are golden.

Squeeze out breadcrumbs and put in a bowl with the onions, bacon, minced meat, herbs, egg and brandy, if used. Season and mix together well.

Cut out eight 5 inch (13 cm) squares of greaseproof paper or aluminium foil. Place a little of the meat mixture in the centre of each, then screw paper or foil together at the top and tie with string. Place on a baking tray and bake for 20 minutes. Serve hot in their wrappings with fresh crusty bread.

Terrine à la maison

Overall timing 3 hours plus overnight marination and chilling

Freezing Suitable

To serve 6–8

1 lb	Piece of veal	450 g
12 oz	Cooked tongue	350 g
8 oz	Belly of pork	225 g
2	Onions	2
2 teasp	Chopped parsley	2x5 ml
½ teasp	Dried thyme	2.5 ml
¼ teasp	Ground allspice	1.25 ml
	Salt and pepper	
5 tbsp	Dry white wine	5x15 ml
5 tbsp	Madeira	5x15 ml
	Sliced pork fat	
	Packet of aspic powder	
1	Bay leaf	1

Mince 8 oz (225 g) each of the veal and tongue with belly pork and peeled onions. Mix with parsley, thyme, allspice, seasoning, wine and Madeira.

Line terrine with slices of pork fat. Cut remaining veal and tongue and a little more pork fat into strips. Reserve a quarter of the pork strips. Arrange on third of mixed meat strips over bottom of terrine. Cover with half minced mixture. Repeat layering, finishing with meat strips. Arrange reserved strips of pork fat over top. Cover and leave overnight.

Preheat the oven to 350°F (180°C) Gas 4. Place terrine in a roasting tin containing 1 inch (2.5 cm) of water and bake for about 2 hours till there is no blood in the juices when pierced with a fine skewer. Cool.

Prepare ½ pint (300 ml) aspic. Carefully remove terrine from mould and remove excess fat from sides and top. Wash mould and replace terrine. Place a bay leaf on top, pour aspic over, cover and chill.

Vegetable terrine

Overall timing 2¼ hours plus overnight soaking and chilling

Freezing Suitable: omit the hard-boiled eggs and garnish after thawing

To serve 10–12

8 oz	Dried haricot beans	225 g
2	Onions	2
3	Cloves	3
11 oz	Fresh breadcrumbs	300 g
¼ pint	Milk	150 ml
12 oz	Carrots	350 g
4 oz	Courgettes	125 g
4 oz	Green beans	125 g
4 oz	Fresh shelled peas	125 g
10	Spring onions	10
6	Hard-boiled eggs	6
4 tbsp	Chopped herbs	4x15 ml
2	Eggs	2
	Salt and pepper	
1 teasp	Ground allspice	5 ml
½ pint	Thick mayonnaise	300 ml

Soak beans overnight; drain. Peel one onion and spike with cloves. Add to beans, cover with water and simmer for 1 hour.

Meanwhile, soak crumbs in milk. Chop carrots, courgettes and beans. Cook vegetables including peas till tender. Drain.

Peel and chop remaining onion. Chop spring onions; shell and chop four hard-boiled eggs. Mix all with breadcrumbs and half herbs.

Preheat the oven to 375°F (190°C) Gas 5. Drain beans. Remove cloves from onion. Purée beans, cooked onion and half vegetables. Beat in crumb mixture, eggs, seasoning, allspice and rest of vegetables. Press into greased and lined 3 pint (1.7 litre) tin and cover. Place in a roasting tin containing hot water and bake for 1 hour. Cool, then chill till firm.

Turn out terrine and garnish with rest of eggs and half mayonnaise. Mix remainder with herbs for sauce.

Halibut in tomato sauce

Overall timing 45 minutes

Freezing Suitable: reheat from frozen in 425°F (220°C) Gas 7 oven for 30 minutes, then add cream and parsley

To serve 4

1 oz	Butter	25 g
1	Onion	1
2	Tomatoes	2
4	Halibut steaks	4
¼ pint	Dry white wine or cider	150 ml
¼ pint	Water	150 ml
	Salt and pepper	
1 teasp	Cornflour	5 ml
2 tbsp	Single cream	2x15 ml
1 tbsp	Chopped parsley	15 ml

Preheat the oven to 425°F (220°C) Gas 7.

Peel and chop onion. Melt butter in a frying pan, add onion and cook gently until golden. Blanch, peel and chop tomatoes. Add to the pan and cook for 5 minutes. Pour mixture into ovenproof dish and place halibut steaks on top. Add wine or cider and water and season with salt and pepper. Cover and cook in oven for 20–30 minutes.

Place halibut steaks on warmed serving dish and keep hot. Pour sauce into small saucepan. Blend the cornflour with 1 tbsp (15 ml) water and stir into the sauce. Boil for 2 minutes, stirring all the time. Remove from heat and stir in cream and parsley. Adjust seasoning. Pour the sauce over the fish and serve immediately with boiled potatoes and a green salad.

Trout baked in wine

Overall timing 55 minutes

Freezing Not suitable

To serve 4

4x1 lb	Trout	4x450g
	Salt and pepper	
2 tbsp	Plain flour	2x15 ml
2 oz	Butter	50g
2 tbsp	Oil	2x15 ml
1	Small onion	1
½ pint	Dry white wine	300 ml
1 teasp	Chopped parsley	5 ml
1 teasp	Chopped fresh tarragon	5 ml
2	Egg yolks	2
4 fl oz	Carton of double cream	113 ml
	Slices of lemon	
	Sprigs of parsley	

Preheat the oven to 350°F (180°C) Gas 4.

Clean trout. Season the flour and roll trout in it till lightly coated. Heat the butter and oil in a frying pan, add the trout and fry for 2–3 minutes each side till browned. Arrange in an ovenproof dish.

Peel and finely chop the onion. Add to the frying pan and fry gently till transparent. Stir in the wine, bring to the boil and boil rapidly till reduced by half. Stir in the herbs, then pour the mixture over the trout. Cover and bake for 20 minutes.

Meanwhile, beat the egg yolks and cream together in a saucepan.

Lift the trout on to a warmed serving dish and keep hot. Strain the cooking liquor into the cream mixture and stir over a low heat, without boiling, till thick enough to coat the back of the spoon. Pour into a warmed sauce-boat.

Garnish the trout with lemon slices and parsley sprigs and serve immediately with the sauce and parsleyed new potatoes.

Fish rolls in whisky sauce

Overall timing 45 minutes

Freezing Not suitable

To serve 4

1	Medium-size onion	1
4 oz	Butter	125 g
¼ pint	Dry white wine	150 ml
¼ pint	Water	150 ml
	Bouquet garni	
8	White fish fillets	8
12 oz	Flat mushrooms	350 g
3 tbsp	Plain flour	3x15 ml
8	Small button mushrooms	8
	Salt and pepper	
4 tbsp	Whisky	4x15 ml
4 fl oz	Carton of single cream	113 ml

Peel and chop onion. Melt 1 oz (25 g) of the butter in a frying pan, add onion and fry till transparent. Remove from the heat and add the wine, water and bouquet garni.

Skin fish fillets. Roll them up and arrange join down in frying pan. Bring to the boil, cover and simmer for about 10 minutes till just tender.

Meanwhile, slice flat mushrooms. Melt 1 oz (25 g) butter in small frying pan, add sliced mushrooms and fry for 5 minutes.

Lift fish out of cooking liquor and arrange on a warmed serving dish. Keep hot. Strain cooking liquor. Melt remaining butter in a saucepan, add flour and cook for 1 minute. Gradually add cooking liquor and bring to the boil, stirring constantly. Add button mushrooms and seasoning and simmer for 3 minutes.

Remove from heat and stir in half whisky and the cream. Spoon sauce over fish. Heat remaining whisky in a ladle. Ignite and add to sliced mushrooms. When the flames die down, season and spoon over the fish.

Grilled herrings with parsley butter

Overall timing 20 minutes

Freezing Not suitable

To serve 4

4 oz	Unsalted butter	125 g
2 tbsp	Chopped parsley	2x15 ml
1 tbsp	Lemon juice	15 ml
4	Cleaned whole herrings	4
1 tbsp	Oil	15 ml
	Salt and pepper	
1	Lemon	1
	Sprigs of parsley	

Mash butter with chopped parsley and lemon juice. Form into a roll, wrap in greaseproof paper and chill till ready to use.

Preheat the grill.

Brush herrings with oil and season. Place on grill pan and cook for 7 minutes on each side.

Arrange herrings on serving plate. Garnish with lemon, pats of chilled butter and parsley sprigs.

Scampi kebabs

Overall timing 25 minutes

Freezing Not suitable

To serve 4

2 lb	Scampi	900 g
	Salt and pepper	
2 oz	Butter	50 g
3 tbsp	Olive oil	3 x 15 ml
3 tbsp	Chopped parsley	3 x 15 ml
6 tbsp	Lemon juice	6 x 15 ml

Preheat grill; line grill pan with foil.

Remove legs and heads from scampi. Wash and dry, then thread on to four skewers. Sprinkle with salt and pepper.

Melt butter with oil, then add parsley and lemon juice. Brush scampi with oil mixture and grill for 5 minutes. Turn skewers, pour over remaining oil mixture and grill for a further 5–7 minutes, basting occasionally.

Place in warmed serving dish, pour over grilling juices and serve immediately with lemon wedges and sauté potatoes.

Braised monkfish

Overall timing 1 hour

Freezing Not suitable

To serve 4

2 lb	Piece of monkfish	900 g
	Salt and pepper	
1 tbsp	Plain flour	15 ml
2 oz	Butter	50 g
8 oz	Onions	225 g
1	Carrot	1
8 oz	Tomatoes	225 g
1	Garlic clove	1
	Bouquet garni	
¼ pint	Dry white wine or fish stock	150 ml

Sprinkle the monkfish with salt and pepper and lightly coat with the flour. Melt the butter in a flameproof casserole. Add the fish and fry over a moderate heat till browned on all sides. Remove from the pan and reserve.

Peel and thinly slice the onions and carrot. Add to the casserole. Fry for 5 minutes till golden brown.

Slice the tomatoes and add to the pan with the peeled and crushed garlic. Return the fish to the pan with the bouquet garni and white wine or fish stock. Cover and simmer for about 30 minutes till the fish is tender.

Discard the bouquet garni. Carefully remove the fish from the pan and place on a warmed serving dish. Arrange the vegetables around the fish and pour the cooking liquor over. Serve immediately with creamed potatoes and baked tomatoes with the skin curled back.

Sole niçoise

Overall timing 35 minutes

Freezing Not suitable

To serve 6

6	Half-sole fillets	6
	Salt and pepper	
2 tbsp	Plain flour	2x15 ml
4 oz	Butter	125 g
1 lb	Large tomatoes	450 g
2	Lemons	2
1	Garlic clove	1
6	Black olives	6
6	Anchovy fillets	6

Preheat grill. Season flour and lightly coat fish. Arrange half fish, skin side up, on grill pan. Melt half butter in a frying pan and brush over fish. Grill for 3–4 minutes.

Turn fish over carefully, brush with butter and grill for a further 3–4 minutes till tender. Arrange on a warmed serving dish and keep hot while you cook the remaining fish.

Meanwhile, blanch, peel and thickly slice tomatoes. Peel one lemon and cut into six slices. Squeeze juice from other lemon. Peel and crush garlic.

Melt remaining butter in frying pan, add garlic, tomatoes and seasoning and cook for 5 minutes.

Heat a flat skewer and press it on to fish to make a decorative pattern. Add lemon juice to tomatoes and spoon over fish. Top with lemon slices. Wrap each olive in an anchovy fillet and garnish fish.

Baked salmon with herbs

Overall timing 50 minutes

Freezing Not suitable

To serve 8

2 oz	Butter	50 g
1	Large onion	1
3	Sage leaves	3
1 tbsp	Chopped parsley	15 ml
4	Thick salmon steaks	4
2 tbsp	Lemon juice	2x15 ml
	Salt and pepper	
	Slices of lemon	
	Flat leafed parsley	

Preheat the oven to 325°F (170°C) Gas 3.

Spread half the butter over centre of a large sheet of foil and place on baking tray. Peel and finely chop the onion and sprinkle over the foil with chopped sage and parsley. Arrange fish steaks on the foil, sprinkle with lemon juice and seasoning, and dot with remaining butter. Bring sides of foil up over the fish and join together well.

Bake for about 35 minutes till salmon is tender. Remove from the oven, arrange on a warmed serving dish and garnish with halved lemon slices and flat leafed parsley. Serve immediately.

Golden fish

Overall timing 1 hour

Freezing Not suitable

To serve 4

1	Slice of onion	1
1	Slice of carrot	1
½	Stalk of celery	½
1	Bay leaf	1
1 lb	Whiting fillets	450 g
½ pint	Thick white sauce	300 ml
2	Egg yolks	2
2	Eggs	2
¼ teasp	Grated nutmeg	1.25 ml
	Salt and pepper	
8	Small fish fillets	8
6 oz	Fresh breadcrumbs	175 g
1 oz	Butter	25 g
4 tbsp	Oil	4x15 ml

Put vegetables and bay leaf in deep frying pan with ½ pint (300 ml) water. Bring to the boil. Skin whiting fillets and add to pan. Cover and simmer for 10 minutes. Drain whiting and purée. Beat into sauce with egg yolks, one egg, nutmeg and seasoning.

Skin small fillets. Spread with sauce mixture and fold in half. Secure with cocktail sticks. Lightly beat remaining egg and brush over fish. Coat with breadcrumbs.

Melt butter with oil in a frying pan, add fish and fry gently for about 8 minutes each side till tender and golden. Drain, remove cocktail sticks and serve hot.

Fish with artichokes

Overall timing 50 minutes

Freezing Not suitable

To serve 4

1½ lb	Waxy potatoes	700 g
	Salt and pepper	
8	White fish fillets	8
6 tbsp	Milk	6x15 ml
4 tbsp	Plain flour	4x15 ml
4 oz	Butter	125 g
14 oz	Can of artichoke hearts	397 g
2	Firm tomatoes	2
2 teasp	Chopped parsley	2x5 ml
2 tbsp	Lemon juice	2x15 ml

Peel and quarter potatoes. Cook in boiling salted water for 10 minutes. Drain. Skin fillets. Brush with milk; coat in seasoned flour.

Melt half butter in a frying pan and fry potatoes till golden all over.

Melt remaining butter in another frying pan and fry fish for about 4 minutes each side.

Drain and quarter artichoke hearts. Add to potatoes and cook for 3 minutes. Slice tomatoes, add to pan in which fish was cooked and cook for 3 minutes. Stir in parsley and lemon juice.

Put potatoes and artichokes in serving dish and top with fish. Garnish with tomatoes; pour pan juices over.

Beef with oranges

Overall timing 1¼ hours

Freezing Not suitable

To serve 6

2¼ lb	Rolled sirloin or piece of rump	1 kg
	Salt and pepper	
	Pinch of dried thyme	
3	Oranges	3
3 tbsp	Oil	3x15 ml
¼ pint	Hot beef stock	150 ml
2 tbsp	Cornflour	2x15 ml
¼ pint	Carton of single cream	150 ml
1 tbsp	Grand Marnier	15 ml
1 tbsp.	Brandy	15 ml

Preheat the oven to 425°F (220°C) Gas 7.

Score fat on beef with a sharp knife, then rub all over with salt, pepper and thyme.

Grate rind of one orange, then squeeze juice from it and from a second orange. Thinly slice third orange.

Heat oil in roasting tin. Add beef and brown on all sides. Add orange juice. Roast for 50–55 minutes, basting at intervals. Place beef on serving dish with orange slices. Leave to stand for 10 minutes.

Meanwhile, make the sauce. Add stock to cooking liquor and cook for a few minutes, then strain into a saucepan. Cool a little and skim off any fat. Mix cornflour with a little water, then stir in half of cream. Add to pan over gentle heat, stirring. Gradually stir in rest of cream, grated orange rind and seasoning. Cook gently for 3 minutes.

Warm Grand Marnier and brandy in a ladle, pour over beef and set alight. Serve with sauce.

Steaks bordelaise

Overall timing 45 minutes

Freezing Not suitable

To serve 4

2	Veal marrow bones, sawn into pieces	2
	Salt and pepper	
1	Onion	1
1	Carrot	1
2 oz	Back bacon	50 g
2 oz	Butter	50 g
3 tbsp	Plain flour	3x15 ml
$\frac{1}{4}$ pint	Chicken stock	150 ml
$\frac{1}{4}$ pint	Red wine	150 ml
	Sprig of thyme	
$\frac{1}{2}$	Bay leaf	$\frac{1}{2}$
4	Fillet or rump steaks	4

Remove marrow from bones. Set aside four slices and finely chop the rest. Lower slices into boiling salted water and leave for 2–3 minutes. Lift out with a draining spoon and reserve.

Peel and finely chop onion and carrot. Derind and chop bacon. Melt butter in a saucepan, add vegetables and bacon and fry for 5 minutes. Stir in flour and cook for 1 minute. Gradually add stock, wine, herbs and seasoning and bring to the boil, stirring. Reduce heat, cover and simmer gently for 20 minutes.

Preheat the grill.

Strain sauce and return to pan. Add chopped marrow and cook gently for a further 10 minutes, stirring frequently.

Season steaks and grill for 1 minute on each side to seal, then a further 2–3 minutes on each side. Place a marrow slice on each steak and grill for 1 more minute.

Arrange steaks on a warmed serving plate. Spoon a little sauce over and pour the rest into a warmed sauce boat.

Beef olives

Overall timing 2½ hours

Freezing Suitable: cook for only 1 hour; complete cooking after thawing

To serve 5

5	Thin slices of braising steak	5
	Salt and pepper	
2 oz	Butter	50 g
20	Button onions	20
3 tbsp	Gin	3x15 ml
1	Garlic clove	1
1 pint	Beer	560 ml
2 tbsp	Tomato purée	2x15 ml
Stuffing		
12 oz	Lean pork	350 g
4 oz	Streaky bacon	125 g
1	Egg	1
½ teasp	Ground allspice	2.5 ml
4	Crushed juniper berries (optional)	4
3 tbsp	Chopped parsley	3x15 ml

To make stuffing, finely mince pork and bacon. Mix with egg, allspice, juniper berries, if used, and half parsley.

Spread out slices of meat and season them lightly. Put some stuffing on each slice and roll up. Tie securely.

Melt butter in flameproof casserole, add peeled onions and cook till golden brown. Remove onions and reserve. Add beef rolls and brown all over, then spoon over gin. Warm and set alight.

When flames die down, stir in peeled and crushed garlic, beer and tomato purée. Bring to the boil, then cover and simmer for 1 hour.

Return onions to pan and simmer uncovered for a further 30 minutes.

Lift beef rolls and onions on to a warmed serving dish. Remove string from rolls, pour over sauce and sprinkle with remaining chopped parsley.

Roast veal with bacon

Overall timing 2¼ hours

Freezing Not suitable

To serve 8

8 oz	Piece of smoked streaky bacon	225 g
3 lb	Boned chump end loin of veal	1.4 kg
	Salt and pepper	
1 tbsp	Oil	15 ml
2 oz	Butter	50 g
2 tbsp	Plain flour	2x15 ml
½ pint	Light stock	300 ml
¼ pint	Dry white wine	150 ml

Preheat the oven to 325°F (170°C) Gas 3.

Derind the bacon, remove the bones and cut into 1 inch (2.5 cm) wide strips. Place the veal on a board and season. Arrange the strips of bacon lengthways along the veal, then roll the meat round the bacon and tie into a neat shape with fine string.

Heat the oil and butter in a flameproof casserole, add the meat and fry over a moderate heat for about 10 minutes, turning, till browned on all sides. Season, cover and cook in the oven for about 1½ hours till the meat juices run clear.

Lift the meat out of the casserole and place on a warmed serving dish. Discard the string and keep the veal hot. Heat the juices in the casserole, add the flour and cook for 1 minute, stirring. Gradually add the stock and wine and bring to the boil, stirring constantly. Simmer for 2 minutes. Taste and adjust seasoning and pour into warmed gravy boat.

Carve the meat into thick slices and serve with the gravy, new potatoes and sliced green beans.

Fillet of veal with mushroom sauce

Overall timing 30 minutes plus marination

Freezing Not suitable

To serve 6

6x4 oz	Pieces of veal fillet	6x125 g
8 oz	Button mushrooms	225 g
1	Small onion	1
3 oz	Butter	75 g
	Salt and pepper	
4 tbsp	Whisky	4x15 ml
¼ pint	White wine or stock	150 ml
4 tbsp	Double cream	4x15 ml
1 teasp	Lemon juice	5 ml
Marinade		
2 tbsp	Olive oil	2x15 ml
1 tbsp	Meaux mustard	15 ml
1 tbsp	Worcestershire sauce	15 ml
	Salt and pepper	

Put veal into a large bowl. Combine marinade ingredients and pour over. Leave for 1½ hours, turning meat from time to time.

Thinly slice mushrooms. Peel and chop onion. Melt 1 oz (25 g) of the butter in a saucepan and fry onion till transparent. Add mushrooms and fry for a further 3 minutes.

Melt remaining butter in a large frying pan and brown veal on both sides. Add seasoning. Heat whisky in a ladle, set alight and pour over veal. When flames die down, add mushroom mixture and wine or stock. Simmer gently for 3 minutes, turning veal once.

Arrange veal on a warmed serving dish and keep hot. Boil sauce for 3 minutes to reduce slightly, then remove from heat and stir in cream and lemon juice. Pour over veal. Serve immediately with sauté potatoes and a crisp mixed salad.

Wiener schnitzel

Overall timing 25 minutes plus chilling

Freezing Suitable: cook after thawing

To serve 4

	Salt	
2 tbsp	Plain flour	2x15 ml
1	Egg	1
2 oz	Breadcrumbs	50 g
4x5 oz	Slices of veal	4x150 g
1 oz	Butter	25 g
2 oz	Pork dripping	50 g
2	Lemons	2
	Sprigs of parsley	

Mix salt and flour together in a bowl. Beat egg in another bowl. Place breadcrumbs in a third bowl. Dip veal slices into flour, then into the egg and finally coat both sides with breadcrumbs. If possible, chill for 30 minutes on a large flat dish to help the egg and crumb layer adhere.

Heat butter and pork dripping in a large frying pan. Add the veal slices two at a time and cook for 2–3 minutes on each side. Place on a warmed serving plate and garnish with lemon slices and parsley. Serve wedges of lemon separately.

Veal escalopes in ginger sauce

Overall timing 40 minutes

Freezing Suitable: reheat from frozen in 325°F (170°C) Gas 3 oven

To serve 4

2	Onions	2
4 tbsp	Oil	4x15 ml
2 tbsp	Lemon juice	2x15 ml
½ teasp	Dried thyme	2.5 ml
	Salt and pepper	
1 teasp	Ground ginger	5 ml
1 lb	Escalopes of veal	450 g
3 tbsp	Plain flour	3x15 ml
1 oz	Butter	25 g
1 tbsp	Tomato purée	15 ml
½ pint	Stock	300 ml
2 oz	Cooked tongue	50 g
1 oz	Cooked ham	25 g
1 oz	Button mushrooms	25 g

Peel and chop the onions. Put into a bowl with 2 tbsp (2x15 ml) of the oil, the lemon juice, thyme, seasoning and ginger. Mix together, then add the veal, cut in half. Marinate for 15–30 minutes.

Remove veal from marinade and dry with kitchen paper. Coat well with 2 tbsp (2x15 ml) of the flour. Heat remaining oil with butter in a frying pan, add veal and cook gently on both sides till brown but not crisp. Remove veal with draining spoon and set aside.

Stir remaining flour into pan, and gradually add tomato purée, strained marinade and stock.

Cut the tongue, ham and mushrooms into fine strips and add to the pan with the veal. Cook for 10 minutes till sauce is thick.

Place in warmed serving dish and serve with rice or thick slices of crusty bread and a crisp green salad.

Sweetbreads Grand Duke

Overall timing 35 minutes

Freezing Not suitable

To serve 4

1 lb	Prepared calves' sweetbreads	450 g
	Salt and pepper	
4 tbsp	Plain flour	4 x 15 ml
2 oz	Butter	50 g
$\frac{1}{4}$ teasp	Grated nutmeg	1.25 ml
1 pint	Cheese sauce (see page 28)	560 ml

Preheat the oven to 425°F (220°C) Gas 7.

Slice the sweetbreads thickly lengthways. Season the flour and toss the sweetbreads in it till evenly coated. Melt the butter in a frying pan, add the sweetbreads and fry gently for 5–10 minutes till tender and golden. Drain the sweetbreads and arrange in a shallow ovenproof dish.

Add the nutmeg to the cheese sauce and spoon over the sweetbreads. Bake for 15 minutes till bubbling and golden.

Crown roast of pork

Overall timing 4 hours

Freezing Not suitable

To serve 12

2	Foreloins of pork each with 6 ribs	2
3 oz	Butter or dripping	75 g
Stuffing		
2	Onions	2
1 oz	Butter	25 g
2	Stalks of celery	2
1	Dessert apple	1
1 lb	Pork sausagemeat	450 g
4 oz	Fresh breadcrumbs	125 g
½ teasp	Dried sage	2.5 ml
2 tbsp	Chopped parsley	2x15 ml
	Salt and pepper	

Trim a ½ inch (12.5 mm) strip of meat from tips of rib bones of each loin. Scrape exposed bones clean. Place loins fat-side down on a board. Make five 1 inch (2.5 cm) deep cuts into meat to create six chops in each loin. Fat-side down, place loins together and sew end rib bones of each loin to make a long strip. Stand strip on board with ribs uppermost and fat inside, and bend loins till ends touch and form a circle. Sew together. Place in roasting tin and season inside and out.

Preheat the oven to 350°F (180°C) Gas 4.

To make stuffing, peel and finely chop onions. Melt butter in a frying pan and fry onions till transparent. Chop celery; peel, core and chop apple. Add to pan and fry for 3 minutes. Tip contents of pan into a bowl and mix in remaining stuffing ingredients. Spoon into centre of crown, pressing it in to keep crown a neat shape, and smooth top into a dome. Wrap a piece of foil around each exposed length of bone to prevent charring.

Put butter or dripping into tin around crown and roast for 2–2½ hours, basting occasionally. Discard foil and top each bone with a cutlet frill to serve.

Pork baked with cheese

Overall timing 2¼ hours

Freezing Not suitable

To serve 8

2 oz	Butter	50 g
3¼ lb	Boned and rolled pork hind loin	1.5 kg
4 oz	Carrots	125 g
4 oz	Onions	125 g
	Salt and pepper	
	Bouquet garni	
12	Slices of Gruyère or Cheddar cheese	12
¼ pint	Water	150 ml
¼ pint	Dry white wine	150 ml

Melt the butter in a large, heavy-based saucepan and brown the pork on all sides. Peel and chop carrots and onions, add to pan and cook for 5 minutes. Season with salt and pepper and add bouquet garni. Cover tightly and cook over very low heat for 1¼–1½ hours (use an asbestos mat, if necessary, to keep the heat low). Turn the joint over halfway through cooking time.

Remove joint from pan and leave to cool. Discard bouquet garni. Preheat oven to 400°F (200°C) Gas 6.

Make 12 deep cuts ¼ inch (6 mm) apart almost through to the base of the joint. Place a slice of cheese into each cut. Season lightly and put in ovenproof dish. Bake for about 15 minutes till cheese melts and starts to brown, and the meat is well heated through.

Meanwhile press contents of pan through a sieve. Return purée to pan with water and bring to boil, stirring. Add wine and cook gently for 5 minutes.

Pour sauce into gravy boat and serve separately. Serve joint garnished with water cress sprigs and halved tomato.

Braised pork with plum sauce

Overall timing 1¾ hours

Freezing Not suitable

To serve 6

2 oz	Lard	50 g
	Salt and pepper	
2½ lb	Boned and rolled loin of pork	1.1 kg
½ pint	Light stock	300 ml
3	Sage leaves	3
2 lb	Small potatoes	900 g
1½ lb	Red plums	700 g
2 oz	Sugar	50 g
1 tbsp	Chopped parsley	15 ml

Preheat the oven to 400°F (200°C) Gas 6.

Melt lard in a roasting tin. Season pork and fry quickly over a high heat till browned on all sides. Pour off the fat and reserve. Add the stock and sage leaves, cover the tin with foil and braise in the oven for 45 minutes.

Meanwhile, peel potatoes. Put into a saucepan, cover with cold salted water and bring to the boil. Drain.

Remove meat from oven and strain stock into a saucepan. Add reserved fat to roasting tin with the potatoes, return to the oven and cook uncovered for a further 50 minutes, basting the meat and potatoes occasionally.

Meanwhile, wash plums. Halve 1 lb (450 g) of them and discard stones. Add to the stock with the sugar. Bring to the boil, then cover and simmer for 10–15 minutes, stirring occasionally. Poach the rest of the plums whole in a little water till tender.

Remove meat from tin, carve into thick slices and arrange on a warmed serving plate. Arrange the potatoes and whole poached plums around the meat. Sprinkle with parsley. Lightly mash remaining plums and pour into a warmed sauceboat.

Pork chops in white wine

Overall timing 45 minutes

Freezing Not suitable

To serve 4

4x5 oz	Pork chops	4x150g
	Salt and pepper	
	Plain flour	
1	Garlic clove	1
1	Sprig of rosemary	1
2 oz	Butter	50g
$\frac{1}{4}$ pint	Dry white wine	150 ml

Preheat the oven to 375°F (190°C) Gas 5.

Trim the excess fat off the chops. Season the flour and use to coat the chops. Peel and crush the garlic. Chop the rosemary.

Melt the butter in a flameproof casserole. Add the garlic and rosemary and stir well. Put the chops in the casserole and cook for 2 minutes on each side. Pour in the wine and enough water to cover the chops. Bring to the boil.

Cover the casserole and place it in the oven. Cook for 30 minutes or until the chops are brown and the liquid has nearly evaporated.

Guard of honour

Overall timing 1½ hours

Freezing Not suitable

To serve 4

2 lb	Best end of neck of lamb	900 g
1 tbsp	Oil	15 ml
1	Garlic clove	1
2 tbsp	Dried breadcrumbs	2x15 ml
2 tbsp	Chopped parsley	2x15 ml
	Salt and pepper	

Have the butcher chine the lamb, and scrape the bone tips free of fat and skin.

Preheat oven to 350°F (180°C) Gas 4.

Place lamb fatty side up in roasting tin with oil. Roast for 30 minutes. Remove from oven.

Peel and crush garlic and place in a bowl with breadcrumbs, parsley and seasoning. Mix well. Spread mixture on to fatty side of the joint, pressing it lightly to make it stick. Cover tips of bones with foil. Stand joint upright in roasting tin.

Return meat to oven and roast for a further 45 minutes, or till tender. Remove the foil and decorate with cutlet frills and watercress. Serve with tomatoes and deep-fried matchstick potatoes.

Lamb cutlets villervi

Overall timing 1 hour

Freezing Not suitable

To serve 6

5 oz	Butter	150 g
6	Best end cutlets of lamb	6
1 tbsp	Marsala	15 ml
2 oz	Plain flour	50 g
¼ pint	Milk	150 ml
	Salt and pepper	
½ teasp	Grated nutmeg	2.5 ml
2 oz	Cooked ham	50 g
1 tbsp	Grated Parmesan cheese	15 ml
2	Egg yolks	2
4 tbsp	Dried breadcrumbs	4x15 ml
2 tbsp	Oil	2x15 ml

Melt 1 oz (25 g) butter in frying pan, add cutlets and quickly brown on both sides. Add Marsala, reduce heat and cook for 5 minutes. Remove cutlets from pan.

Melt 2 oz (50 g) butter in saucepan. Stir in the flour and cook for 1 minute. Gradually stir in the milk, then add seasoning and nutmeg. Bring to the boil, stirring, and cook for 3 minutes. Remove from heat and plunge pan into cold water to cool contents quickly. Finely chop ham and add to pan with cheese and egg yolks. Mix well.

Sprinkle the breadcrumbs on to a baking tray. Dip cutlets in the thick sauce and then in the crumbs, pressing them on to the coating of sauce.

Heat remaining butter and oil in frying pan till frothy. Add cutlets and cook for 5–10 minutes on each side or until crisp and golden. Arrange cutlets on warmed serving dish, garnish with parsley and serve with cauliflower florets in butter sauce.

Pâté-stuffed roast lamb

Overall timing 2½ hours

Freezing Not suitable

To serve 6–8

3 lb	Boned shoulder of lamb	1.4 kg
	Salt and pepper	
4 oz	Button mushrooms	125 g
4 oz	Butter	125 g
4 oz	Liver pâté	125 g
2 tbsp	Chopped parsley	2x15 ml
¼ pint	Stock	150 ml
3 tbsp	Dry sherry	3x15 ml
4 tbsp	Double cream	4x15 ml

Preheat the oven to 350°F (180°C) Gas 4.

Flatten meat and season both sides. Thinly slice mushrooms. Melt half the butter in frying pan, add mushrooms and cook for 5 minutes or till light golden.

Beat pâté until smooth and spread over meat. Cover with the mushrooms and parsley. Season. Roll meat up and secure at regular intervals with string. Spread with remaining butter. Place in flameproof casserole and brown quickly on all sides. Pour stock over and roast in oven for 1½–2 hours till tender.

Lift meat out of casserole. Remove string and slice the meat. Arrange slices on a warmed serving dish. Keep hot. Place casserole containing juices over the heat and bring to the boil, stirring. Remove from the heat and stir in the sherry and cream. Taste and adjust seasoning. Pour into a sauce boat and serve with lamb.

Lamb cutlets in pastry

Overall timing 1¼ hours

Freezing Suitable: bake after thawing

To serve 4

7½ oz	Frozen puff pastry	212 g
4	Large lamb cutlets	4
1 tbsp	Oil	15 ml
	Salt and pepper	
2 oz	Mint jelly	50 g
1	Egg	1

Thaw pastry. Preheat the oven to 425°F (220°C) Gas 7.

Trim the cutlets, cleaning 1 inch (2.5 cm) down from the tip of the bone end and removing excess fat. Heat the oil in a frying pan and fry the cutlets quickly for about 2 minutes on each side to sear them. Remove, drain on kitchen paper and cool.

Rub the cutlets with salt and pepper, then spread the mint jelly over one side of each cutlet.

On a well-floured surface roll out dough to an oblong, 6 inches x 20 inches (15 cm x 50 cm). Cut into four equal strips and brush lightly with beaten egg. Wind each dough strip, egg side outside, around a cutlet, starting at the thin end and overlapping each previous "turn"; pinch to seal.

Brush again with beaten egg and place on a greased baking tray. Bake for about 30 minutes till golden.

Alsatian chicken

Overall timing 1½ hours

Freezing Not suitable

To serve 4–6

8	Chicken legs and wings	8
1	Garlic clove	1
2 oz	Streaky bacon	50 g
4 tbsp	Oil	4x15 ml
2	Onions	2
8 fl oz	Dry white wine	225 ml
4 oz	Mushrooms	125 g
2	Bay leaves	2
2 tbsp	Chopped parsley	2x15 ml
2 tbsp	Chopped chives	2x15 ml
	Salt and pepper	
1 tbsp	Arrowroot	15 ml
¼ pint	Carton of single cream	150 ml
	Sprigs of fresh parsley	

Rub chicken all over with halved garlic clove. Derind and dice bacon. Fry in flameproof casserole till brown. Add oil and when hot brown chicken pieces on all sides.

Peel and finely chop onions. Add to casserole and brown. Pour in half of wine, cover and cook for 35 minutes.

Slice mushrooms and add to casserole with bay leaves, half the chopped parsley and chives and seasoning. Cover and cook for 10 minutes.

Discard bay leaves. Take out chicken pieces with a draining spoon and place on a warmed serving dish. Keep hot. If there's a lot of liquid in casserole, boil till reduced by half. Mix arrowroot with remaining wine and stir into pan juices. Cook, stirring, till sauce thickens, then gradually stir in cream. When hot (it must not boil) pour sauce over chicken. Garnish with remaining chopped parsley and chives and parsley sprigs.

Pastry-wrapped stuffed chicken

Overall timing 2¼ hours

Freezing Not suitable

To serve 4

3 lb	Ovenready chicken	1.4 kg
	Salt	
1 oz	Butter	25 g
12 oz	Shortcrust pastry	350 g
1	Egg	1
Stuffing		
8 oz	Mushrooms	225 g
1 oz	Butter	25 g
2 tbsp	Sherry	2x15 ml
	Salt and pepper	
6 oz	Chicken livers	175 g
1	Small onion	1
2 oz	Dried breadcrumbs	50 g

First make stuffing. Slice mushrooms. Melt butter in a pan and fry mushrooms for 3 minutes. Add sherry and cook for 3 minutes. Season with salt and pepper.

Finely chop chicken livers. Peel and finely chop onion. Add both to pan with breadcrumbs and mix well. Heat gently for 5 minutes.

Season chicken inside and out with salt. Stuff with liver mixture and close the opening. Melt butter in a roasting tin and brown chicken on all sides for 20 minutes.

Preheat the oven to 400°F (200°C) Gas 6.

Roll out dough on a lightly floured surface till about ¼ inch (6 mm) thick and large enough to wrap round chicken. Remove chicken from roasting tin. Drain and allow to cool slightly, then place, breast side down, on dough. Moisten edges and wrap dough round chicken. Press edges together well.

Place chicken on greased baking tray with seam underneath. Use dough trimmings to decorate top. Brush with beaten egg and bake for 1½–1¾ hours. If pastry shows signs of overbrowning, cover with foil.

Chicken supreme

Overall timing 2 hours

Freezing Not suitable

To serve 4

2	Carrots	2
2	Onions	2
2	Leeks	2
1	Stalk of celery	1
	Salt	
2½ pints	Water or stock	1.5 litres
3 lb	Ovenready chicken	1.4 kg
½	Lemon	½
8 oz	Rice	225 g
Sauce		
2 oz	Butter	50 g
1 tbsp	Plain flour	15 ml
2	Egg yolks	2
2 tbsp	Single cream	2x15 ml
	Salt and pepper	

Peel carrots and onions. Chop leeks and celery. Bring salted water or stock to the boil in a flameproof casserole, add prepared vegetables and cook for 15 minutes.

Rub chicken with the lemon. Add to casserole, cover and simmer gently for 1 hour. (If you prefer, chicken joints can be used instead of a whole chicken – they need only to be cooked for 45 minutes.)

Measure out 1 pint (560 ml) stock from casserole and place in a saucepan. Continue cooking chicken for a further 15 minutes. Bring stock in saucepan to the boil, add rice and cook for 15 minutes.

Meanwhile, prepare sauce. Melt butter in a saucepan and stir in flour. Measure out another 1 pint (560 ml) stock from casserole and gradually stir into pan. Cook, stirring till thickened. Remove from heat and stir in egg yolks and then cream. Season.

Drain rice and place on warmed serving dish. Remove chicken from casserole, cut into portions and arrange on top of rice. Pour sauce over and serve.

Chicken Kiev

Overall timing 1¼ hours

Freezing Suitable: egg, crumb and fry after thawing

To serve 4

4 oz	Softened butter	125 g
2 tbsp	Lemon juice	2x15 ml
1	Garlic clove	1
1 tbsp	Chopped parsley	15 ml
	Salt and pepper	
4	Boneless chicken breasts	4
	Oil for frying	
3 tbsp	Plain flour	3x15 ml
1	Egg	1
3 tbsp	Fresh white breadcrumbs	3x15 ml

Work together the butter and lemon juice until smooth. Peel and crush the garlic and add to the butter with the parsley and seasoning. Mix well. Shape into a cylinder, wrap in foil and place in freezer for 1 hour to firm.

Place the chicken breasts between two sheets of dampened greaseproof paper on a flat surface and beat flat with a heavy knife or wooden mallet until thin.

Heat the oil in a deep-fryer to 350°F (170°C).

Place a piece of butter on each chicken breast. Roll chicken round butter and secure with a cocktail stick. Coat each piece of chicken all over with the flour, then dip in the beaten egg to cover and finally in the breadcrumbs, pressing them on well. Fry for 12–15 minutes until golden brown. Drain on kitchen paper, remove cocktail sticks and serve immediately with lemon wedges and a green salad.

Duck with oranges

Overall timing 2 hours

Freezing Not suitable

To serve 4

4 lb	Ovenready duck	1.8 kg
	Salt and pepper	
½ pint	Hot chicken stock	300 ml
2 teasp	Caster sugar	2x5 ml
2 tbsp	White wine vinegar	2x15 ml
4	Oranges	4

Preheat the oven to 400°F (200°C) Gas 6.

Prick duck all over with a fork. Season well and place on rack in roasting tin. Roast for 45 minutes till brown and crisp.

Remove all but 1 tbsp (15 ml) of the fat from the tin. Pour hot stock over duck. Cover and roast for a further 30 minutes till cooked.

Heat sugar gently in a pan until it caramelizes, then remove from heat and add vinegar. Remove duck and strain juices from roasting tin into sugar mixture. Replace duck in tin and keep warm.

Cut the rind from one orange into thin matchsticks. Squeeze the juice from two oranges and add to the pan with the rind. Cook gently for 5 minutes till the rind has softened.

Remove duck from oven and cut into portions. Arrange on warmed serving dish and spoon over a little of the orange sauce. Peel and segment remaining oranges and use to garnish duck. Serve with sautéed potatoes and peas, and with the rest of the sauce served in a sauce or gravy boat.

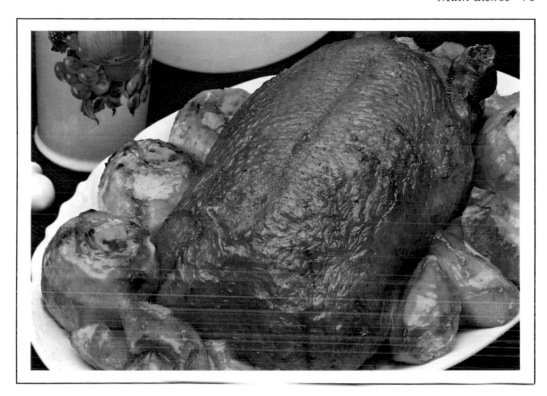

Duck with apples and cream

Overall timing 1 hour 20 minutes

Freezing Not suitable

To serve 4

3½ lb	Ovenready duck	1.6 kg
	Salt and pepper	
6	Granny Smith apples	6
1 oz	Butter	25 g
½ pint	Carton of single cream	284 ml

Preheat the oven to 400°F (200°C) Gas 6.

Sprinkle duck inside and out with salt and pepper. Prick all over with a fork and place on wire rack in roasting tin. Roast for 20 minutes, then reduce heat to 350°F (180°C) Gas 4.

Peel and core the apples. Cut two of them into quarters and leave the rest whole. Arrange around the duck, dot with butter and continue roasting for 1 hour or till tender.

Remove duck and apples from the tin. Place duck on serving plate. Keep hot. Pour off excess fat from pan juices, then stir in the cream. Replace apples in tin and baste thoroughly with the sauce. Cook for a further 5 minutes.

Arrange apples round duck. Spoon some sauce over. Serve rest separately.

Flambéed goose

Overall timing 2 hours

Freezing Not suitable

To serve 6

2 tbsp	Oil	2x15 ml
8 lb	Goose (cut into portions	3.6 kg
6 tbsp	Rum	6x15 ml
½ pint	Hot chicken or vegetable stock	300 ml
	Bouquet garni	
	Salt and pepper	
1½ lb	Cooking apples	700 g
2 oz	Butter	50 g
2 tbsp	Caster sugar	2x15 ml
	Grated nutmeg	

Heat the oil in flameproof casserole, add goose portions and brown on all sides. Drain off excess fat.

Warm 4 tbsp (4x15 ml) of the rum in a ladle, set alight and pour, flaming, over the goose. Add hot stock, bouquet garni and seasoning. Cover and cook over a low heat for 1–1½ hours till tender.

Meanwhile, peel, core and thickly slice the apples. Melt butter in a small pan and fry apples till golden. Sprinkle with sugar and cook over a high heat for a few minutes until apples are pulpy, shaking the pan frequently to prevent sticking.

Heat remaining rum in ladle, set alight and pour over apples. Season with salt, pepper and a pinch of grated nutmeg.

Remove goose portions from casserole, place on warmed serving dish and keep hot. Skim surface of fat, then boil to reduce cooking liquor to about ¼ pint (150 ml). Spoon cooking liquor over goose portions and serve with the apple purée and jacket potatoes and garnished with watercress.

Grilled grouse with Marsala sauce

Overall timing 1 hour

Freezing Not suitable

To serve 4

2	Grouse	2
2 tbsp	Oil	2x15 ml
	Salt and pepper	
2 oz	Back bacon	50 g
1	Small onion	1
2 oz	Butter	50 g
1 tbsp	Plain flour	15 ml
¼ pint	Stock	150 ml
4 tbsp	Marsala	4x15 ml
1	Bay leaf	1
4	Thick slices of bread	4

Preheat grill. Clean birds, then cut each one in half along breastbone with poultry shears Rub each piece with oil and sprinkle with salt. Place on grill pan, bony side up, and cook for about 10 minutes, turning once.

Derind and chop bacon. Peel and chop onion. Melt butter in saucepan, add bacon and onion and fry for 5 minutes. Add flour and cook for 2 minutes, then gradually add the stock and Marsala. Bring to the boil, stirring. Add the bay leaf, seasoning, and the cooking juices from the grill pan. Cook over a moderate heat for about 20 minutes, stirring occasionally. Discard bay leaf, then sieve and season to taste.

Toast slices of bread until golden. Place in warmed serving dish and put half a grouse on each. Top with a little sauce and place the rest in a gravy boat. Serve immediately with creamed potatoes and Brussels sprouts.

Cold strawberry soufflé

Overall timing 45 minutes plus chilling

Freezing Suitable: decorate after thawing

To serve 6

4 tbsp	Water	4x15 ml
2 tbsp	Powdered gelatine	2x15 ml
2 lb	Strawberries	900 g
6 oz	Caster sugar	175 g
2	Lemons	2
3	Egg whites	3
½ pint	Carton of double cream	284 ml

Tie a collar of double greaseproof paper or foil round the outside of a 5 inch (13 cm) soufflé dish, 2 inches (5 cm) above rim.

Put the water into a bowl, sprinkle gelatine over and leave to sponge.

Hull strawberries; reserve seven for decoration and sieve the rest. Put half the fruit purée into a pan with the gelatine and sugar. Squeeze juice from lemons and add. Stir over a gentle heat until sugar and gelatine dissolve. Remove from heat and stir in the remaining fruit purée. Leave to cool.

Whisk the egg whites till stiff. In another bowl, whip the cream till stiff. Fold all but 3 tbsp (3x15 ml) of the cream and the egg whites into the strawberry mixture. Turn into prepared dish and chill until firm.

Carefully remove collar. If you like, stir 2 oz (50 g) finely chopped almonds and a few drops of green food colouring together and press on to the exposed edges of the soufflé with a palette knife. Decorate with the reserved cream and halved strawberries.

Angel pie

Overall timing 20 minutes plus 1 hour chilling time

Freezing Not suitable

To serve 6

4	Large egg whites	4
	Pinch of salt	
2 teasp	Wine vinegar	2x5 ml
1 teasp	Vanilla essence	5 ml
8 oz	Caster sugar	225 g
½ pint	Carton of double cream	284 ml
4 oz	Plain or bitter chocolate	125 g
2 tbsp	Icing sugar	2x15 ml
	Chocolate ice cream	

Preheat oven to 300°F (150°C) Gas 2.

Whisk egg whites with salt till soft peaks form. Add vinegar and essence and whisk again, then gradually whisk in caster sugar till mixture is very stiff and will hold its shape.

Pipe an 8 inch (20 cm) round on rice paper on a baking tray. Change nozzle and pipe rosettes at edge of round to make a hollow case.

Bake for 1½ hours. Cool.

About 1 hour before serving, chill cream. Coarsely grate the chocolate.

Remove cream from refrigerator. It should have the consistency of custard. If it is too thick, add a few drops of cold water. Whip cream till thick, gradually adding icing sugar.

Fill the meringue case with chocolate ice cream, then spoon the whipped cream over it. Sprinkle generously with the grated chocolate. Serve immediately.

Oranges Chantilly

Overall timing 10 minutes plus chilling

Freezing Not suitable

To serve 4

½ pint	Carton of double cream	284 ml
1 tbsp	Cold milk	15 ml
1	Ice cube	1
2½ oz	Caster sugar	65 g
1 tbsp	Cointreau	15 ml
4	Large oranges	4

Put the cream, milk and ice cube in a bowl and beat slowly, incorporating as much air into cream as you can. When cream thickens add ½ oz (15 g) sugar and Cointreau and beat till mixture holds soft peaks and is light.

Cut off the tops of oranges, using a small, sharp knife to give a decorative effect, and set aside. Remove flesh with a sharp knife, chop and sprinkle with remaining sugar. Grate rind from the orange tops.

Fill orange shells with flesh, top with orange cream mixture and decorate with grated rind.

Chocolate kisses

Overall timing 1¾ hours

Freezing Suitable: sandwich with cream after thawing

Makes about 20

4	Egg whites	4
2 teasp	White wine vinegar	2x5 ml
1 teasp	Vanilla essence	5 ml
	Pinch of salt	
8 oz	Caster sugar	225 g
1 tbsp	Cocoa powder	15 ml
½ pint	Carton of double cream	284 ml
1 oz	Plain chocolate	25 g

Preheat the oven to 300°F (150°C) Gas 2.

Put egg whites, vinegar, essence and salt in mixing bowl and beat till stiff peaks form. Gradually beat in 6 oz (175 g) of the sugar till mixture is glossy. Gently fold in sifted cocoa and remaining sugar mixed together. Spoon into piping bag fitted with star nozzle and pipe 1¼ inch (3 cm) diameter swirls on to baking trays lined with dampened grease-proof paper. Bake for 1½ hours until dry. Cool on wire rack.

Just before serving whip cream. Grate chocolate and fold into cream. Pipe on to half meringues, and place remainder on top to "kiss" cream.

Coffee cream dessert

Overal timing 55 minutes plus chilling

Freezing Not suitable

To serve 4

1 pint	Milk	560 ml
1	Vanilla pod	1
2 tbsp	Instant coffee powder	2x15 ml
2 oz	Caster sugar	50 g
4	Eggs	4
¼ pint	Carton of whipping cream	150 ml
2 tbsp	Icing sugar	2x15 ml
2 oz	Plain chocolate	50 g

Preheat the oven to 400°F (200°C) Gas 6.

Put milk, vanilla pod, coffee and caster sugar in a saucepan. Bring to the boil, then remove from heat and leave to infuse for 10 minutes. Discard vanilla pod.

Separate two eggs. Beat yolks with remaining whole eggs. Gradually beat in milk mixture. Strain into greased 1 pint (560 ml) mould. Place in roasting tin half-filled with hot water and bake for 45 minutes till set. Cool, then chill for 6 hours.

Whisk egg whites till stiff. Whip cream with icing sugar till holding soft peaks, then fold in egg whites.

Turn out dessert on to serving plate. Pipe cream round. Coarsely grate chocolate and decorate dessert.

Cassata

Overall timing 1¾ hours

Freezing See method

To serve 8

1 pint	Vanilla ice cream	560 ml
1 pint	Chocolate ice cream	560 ml
½ pint	Tutti-frutti ice cream	300 ml

Chill 2½ pint (1.5 litre) bombe mould or pudding basin. Soften vanilla ice cream in refrigerator for 15–20 minutes, then spoon two-thirds into mould. Press it firmly to cover shape of mould. Place remaining vanilla ice cream and mould in freezer and leave till firm. Meanwhile, soften chocolate ice cream in refrigerator.

Take mould out of freezer and press in layer of chocolate ice cream following shape of mould and leaving space in middle. Return mould to freezer and leave for 20 minutes. Meanwhile, soften remaining vanilla ice cream.

Spread vanilla ice cream over chocolate layer, leaving space in middle, and return to freezer for 20 minutes. Meanwhile, soften tutti-frutti ice cream.

Remove mould from freezer and fill centre with tutti-frutti ice cream. Smooth surface. Cover with lid or foil and freeze till firm.

Place mould in refrigerator and leave for 30 minutes. Dip mould in hot water for a few seconds to loosen ice cream. Turn out on to plate.

Champagne sorbet

Overall timing 20 minutes plus freezing

Freezing See method

To serve 6

8 oz	Caster sugar	225 g
1 pint	Water	560 ml
¼ pint	Champagne or dry cider	150 ml
1 tbsp	Lemon juice	15 ml
2	Egg whites	2

Put the sugar and water in a pan and heat gently, stirring until sugar dissolves. Bring to the boil and simmer for 10 minutes without stirring. Do not let the mixture colour. Remove from the heat and cool.

Add the Champagne or cider and lemon juice to the syrup, then pour into a 2 pint (1.1 litre) freezer tray. Freeze till mushy.

Remove mixture from freezer, turn into a bowl and beat well to break down any ice crystals. Whisk the egg whites until stiff and fold into the mixture. Return to the freezer tray and freeze till firm.

Pears in chocolate sauce

Overall timing 40 minutes plus chilling

Freezing Not suitable

To serve 6

6	Firm pears	6
¾ pint	Water	400 ml
1 tbsp	Lemon juice	15 ml
4 oz	Caster sugar	125 g
1	Vanilla pod	1
3½ oz	Plain dessert chocolate	100 g
½ oz	Butter	15 g
	Vanilla ice cream	
	Crystallized violets (optional)	

Peel the pears and remove the stalks. Put the water, lemon juice, sugar and vanilla pod into a saucepan and heat gently till the sugar dissolves. Bring the syrup to the boil, add the pears and simmer for about 15 minutes till just tender. Leave pears to cool in the syrup, then lift them out with a draining spoon and chill for several hours. Reserve the syrup.

Break the chocolate into small pieces and put into a heatproof bowl with the butter. Stand the bowl over a pan of simmering water and stir till melted. Remove from the heat and beat in 2 tbsp (2x15 ml) of the pear syrup.

Arrange the pears in a serving dish and place scoops of ice cream between them. Decorate with crystallized violets, if liked. Spoon the chocolate sauce over the pears and serve.

Oranges in caramel

Overall timing 30 minutes plus maceration

Freezing Not suitable

To serve 4

4	Large oranges	4
8 oz	Caster sugar	225 g
2	Cloves	2
12 fl oz	Water	350 ml
3 tbsp	Cointreau	3x15 ml
4	Crystallized violets	4

Pare the rind from two oranges with a potato peeler. Shred rind into fine long strands and blanch in boiling water for 5 minutes. Drain and rinse in cold water, then dry on kitchen paper.

Put the sugar into a saucepan with the cloves and water and heat, stirring, till dissolved. Bring to the boil and boil rapidly, without stirring, till a golden caramel colour.

Meanwhile, peel the remaining oranges, collecting any juice. Place all oranges in flat-bottom dish with shredded rind.

Remove caramel from the heat. Carefully add the Cointreau and any orange juice, and stir over a low heat to dissolve the caramel. Pour over the oranges and leave to macerate for 3 hours, turning the oranges and rind in the caramel occasionally.

Arrange the oranges on individual serving plates and spoon the caramel over. Pile the shredded rind on to the oranges and decorate each with a crystallized violet, and an orange leaf, if liked. Serve with pouring cream.

Raspberries jubilee

Overall timing 10 minutes plus 2 hours maceration

Freezing Not suitable

To serve 6

12 oz	Fresh or frozen raspberries	350 g
2–4 oz	Caster sugar	50–125 g
3 tbsp	Lemon juice	3 x 15 ml
1½ pints	Vanilla ice cream	850 ml
3 tbsp	Kirsch or brandy	3 x 15 ml

Put raspberries, sugar (add according to taste) and lemon juice in a bowl and macerate for 2 hours in the refrigerator. Chill serving plate.

Transfer raspberries and soaking juices to a saucepan and heat through gently.

Remove ice cream from freezer and place on serving plate. Spoon raspberries and syrup over. Warm Kirsch or brandy in ladle. Set alight and pour over ice cream. Serve immediately.

Raspberry charlotte

Overall timing 50 minutes plus chilling

Freezing Not suitable

To serve 6

1¼ lb	Raspberries	600 g
3 oz	Caster sugar	75 g
1 tbsp	Powdered gelatine	15 ml
8 tbsp	Water	8x15 ml
4 tbsp	Raspberry liqueur or sherry	4x15 ml
24	Sponge fingers	24
½ pint	Carton of double cream	284 ml
1 tbsp	Icing sugar	15 ml

Reserve 8 oz (225 g) of the raspberries for decoration and put the rest into a blender with the caster sugar. Blend to a purée, then press through a nylon sieve into a bowl.

Put the gelatine in a small heatproof bowl with 4 tbsp (4x15 ml) of the water and leave to sponge. Stand bowl in a pan of simmering water and heat, stirring occasionally, till gelatine dissolves. Remove from heat and leave to cool.

Meanwhile, mix together the raspberry liqueur or sherry and remaining water in a bowl. Quickly dip the sponge fingers one at a time into the liquid without soaking them. Use to line bottom and sides of a 2½ pint (1.5 litre) charlotte mould, trimming the ends if necessary.

Trickle the gelatine into the raspberry purée in a thin stream, then fold in carefully. Whip the cream till soft peaks form, then fold gently into the raspberry mixture. Pour into mould and smooth the top.

Chill for several hours, preferably overnight. Run a knife round the edge of the charlotte and turn out on to a serving dish. Sift icing sugar over top and decorate with reserved raspberries.

Melon on the rocks

Overall timing 15 minutes plus chilling

Freezing Not suitable

To serve 4

2	Ripe cantaloup, ogen or honeydew melons	2
2 tbsp	Caster sugar	2x15 ml
4 tbsp	Rum, Kirsch or Maraschino	4x15 ml
	Crushed ice	

Cut the melons into quarters and discard the seeds. Remove the flesh and cut into neat chunks. Put into a glass bowl and sprinkle with sugar. Mix gently and chill for at least 2 hours.

Pour the rum, Kirsch or Maraschino over the melon and mix well. Divide between individual glass dishes and serve immediately on a bed of crushed ice.

Croquembouche

Overall timing 1¼ hours

Freezing Not suitable

To serve 8–12

4 oz	Choux paste	125 g
10 oz	Sugar	275 g
6	Egg yolks	6
6 tbsp	Plain flour	6x15 ml
¾ pint	Hot milk	400 ml
2 oz	Butter	50 g
2 teasp	Vanilla essence	2x5 ml
2 tbsp	Water	2x15 ml

Preheat the oven to 425°F (220°C) Gas 7.

Use two teaspoons to shape small even mounds of choux paste on greased baking trays – make about 36. Bake for about 25 minutes till golden and crisp. Cool on a wire rack and slit buns to release steam.

Beat 6 oz (175 g) sugar with egg yolks till pale and thick. Beat in the flour till smooth. Pour almost boiling milk in steadily, whisking all the time till frothy. Pour into saucepan and heat, stirring, till thick and smooth. Remove from heat and beat in butter and essence. Put saucepan in cold water and cool, stirring from time to time to prevent skin forming.

Spoon custard into a piping bag fitted with a small plain nozzle. Pipe into choux buns.

Dissolve remaining sugar in water in a heavy-based pan without stirring. Tilt pan occasionally. When slightly coloured, remove from heat. Dip buns, one at a time, into caramel with tongs. Arrange nine or ten buns, caramel side up, in a ring on a plate or foil. Slowly build up a cone shape with remaining buns. Carefully lift croquembouche on to serving plate.

Strawberry vacherin

Overall timing 2¼ hours plus cooling

Freezing Not suitable

To serve 8

6	Egg whites	6
12 oz	Caster sugar	350 g
1 lb	Strawberries	450 g
Crème Chantilly		
½ pint	Carton of double cream	284 ml
1 tbsp	Cold milk	15 ml
1	Ice cube	1
1 tbsp	Caster sugar	15 ml
¼ teasp	Vanilla essence	1.25 ml

Preheat the oven to 300°F (150°C) Gas 2.

Line two baking trays with non-stick paper. Draw a 10 inch (25 cm) square on one, and a 6 inch (15 cm) square on the other.

Whisk egg whites till stiff and dry. Sprinkle over 2 tbsp (2×15 ml) of the sugar and whisk in, then gradually whisk in remaining sugar to make a stiff, glossy meringue.

Using the marked squares as a guide, put large spoonfuls of meringue on to paper to make two squares with scalloped edges. Swirl into peaks. Place large square in centre of oven with small square below. Bake for about 1¼ hours till slightly browned and crisp. Cool.

Meanwhile, hull strawberries. To make the Crème Chantilly, whip cream with milk, ice cube, sugar and vanilla essence till it forms soft peaks. Chill till required.

Just before serving, carefully peel the paper from the meringue squares and place the large one on a flat board or serving dish. Spread or pipe two-thirds of the Crème Chantilly over and arrange two-thirds of the strawberries on top. Place the small meringue square on top and spread with the remaining crème. Decorate with remaining strawberries and serve immediately.

Gâteau St. Honoré

Overall timing 1¼ hours

Freezing Not suitable

To serve 8

4 oz	Choux paste	125 g
	Vanilla essence	
8 oz	Shortcrust pastry	225 g
1 pint	Whipping cream	560 ml
2 tbsp	Icing sugar	2x15 ml
3 oz	Caster sugar	75 g
2 tbsp	Water	2x15 ml
	Glacé cherries	
	Angelica	

Preheat the oven to 425°F (220°C) Gas 7.

Prepare the choux paste, adding a few drops of vanilla essence after the eggs.

Roll out the shortcrust dough and cut out a 10 inch (25 cm) round. Place on greased and floured baking tray. Put choux paste into a piping bag, fitted with a small, plain nozzle, and pipe 12 small buns about 1 inch (2.5 cm) in diameter round edge of shortcrust round. Pipe 12 more buns on to the baking tray. Bake for 40 minutes till firm and golden brown. Cool. Make a slit in the side of each bun to release steam.

Whip cream with ½ teasp (2.5 ml) vanilla essence and icing sugar till thick. Use to fill buns and put rest in centre of ring.

Dissolve caster sugar in water and cook till mixture begins to thicken and colour. Spoon a little over buns on pastry. Using tongs, dip remaining buns in caramel and arrange them, caramel-side up, on top of the buns on the shortcrust base.

As caramel cooks, draw up threads with two forks and place on gâteau with whole glacé cherries and strips of angelica, radiating from the centre.

Black Forest gâteau

Overall timing 1¾ hours

Freezing Suitable

To serve 12

6	Eggs	6
6 tbsp	Hand-hot water	6x15 ml
5 oz	Caster sugar	150g
	Salt	
2 oz	Plain flour	50g
3 oz	Cornflour	75g
2 oz	Cocoa powder	50g
2x15 oz	Cans of pitted black cherries	2x425g
2 teasp	Arrowroot	2x5 ml
8 tbsp	Kirsch or brandy	8x15 ml
1½ pints	Double cream	900 ml
2 tbsp	Icing sugar	2x15 ml
2 oz	Plain chocolate	50g

Preheat the oven to 350°F (180°C) Gas 4.

Separate eggs. Beat yolks with water and caster sugar till pale and thick. Whisk whites with pinch of salt till stiff. Fold into yolks. Sift flour with cornflour and cocoa and fold into egg mixture. Pour into greased and lined 9 inch (23 cm) round cake tin. Bake for 1 hour. Cool.

Drain cherries, saving juice. Set aside 12 cherries; chop remainder and cook with 150 ml (¼ pint) juice, the arrowroot and half Kirsch or brandy till thick. Cool.

Cut sponge into three layers. Whip cream with icing sugar and rest of Kirsch or brandy. Use two-fifths of cream and cherry sauce to sandwich sponge layers. Cover top and sides with another two-fifths of cream.

Grate chocolate coarsely. Use to decorate gâteau with remaining cream and reserved cherries.

Praline cream gâteau

Overall timing 1½ hours

Freezing Not suitable

To serve 12

5	Eggs	5
7 oz	Caster sugar	200 g
2 tbsp	Hot water	2x15 ml
5 oz	Plain flour	150 g
2 teasp	Baking powder	2x5 ml
4 oz	Ground hazelnuts	125 g
Filling and topping		
2 oz	Shelled almonds	50 g
6 oz	Granulated sugar	175 g
4 fl oz	Water	120 ml
	Cream of tartar	
1 pint	Double cream	560 ml
½ teasp	Vanilla essence	2.5 ml
1 tbsp	Caster sugar	15 ml

Preheat the oven to 400°F (200°C) Gas 6.

Beat eggs with sugar and hot water till pale and thick. Sift in flour and baking powder, add nuts and fold in gently. Divide between two greased and lined 9 inch (23 cm) sandwich tins and bake for about 30 minutes.

Chop almonds and place on baking tray. Brown in oven for a few minutes. Dissolve granulated sugar in water and cook till golden brown. Remove from heat. Stir in pinch of cream of tartar and almonds and pour at once on to oiled baking tray. Immediately mark into 13 triangles with a knife dipped into hot water and leave to set.

Cut out triangles. Put rest of praline in plastic bag and crush. Whip cream with essence and caster sugar till stiff. Divide in half; add half crushed praline to one portion.

Cut each cake into two layers, then sandwich together with praline cream. Spread two-thirds of plain cream over top and sides of cake. Mark the top into 12 slices with a knife. Pipe rest of cream in a large rosette on each slice. Put praline triangles on rosettes. Press remaining crushed praline on to side of cake and sprinkle a little over top.

Chocolate rum gâteau

Overall timing 1½ hours plus cooling

Freezing Suitable: ice after thawing

To serve 16

4 oz	Cocoa powder	125 g
7 tbsp	Rum	7x15 ml
10 oz	Butter	275 g
1 lb 2 oz	Granulated sugar	500 g
4	Eggs	4
1 teasp	Vanilla essence	5 ml
14 oz	Plain flour	400 g
	Salt	
2 teasp	Bicarbonate of soda	2x5 ml
½ teasp	Baking powder	2.5 ml
4 tbsp	Apricot jam	4x15 ml
3½ oz	Plain chocolate	100 g
4 oz	Icing sugar	125 g

Preheat the oven to 350°F (180°C) Gas 4.

Mix cocoa with 16 fl oz (450 ml) boiling water and 1 tbsp (15 ml) rum, then cool. Cream 8 oz (225 g) butter and granulated sugar till pale and fluffy. Gradually beat in eggs. Add essence. Sift flour with soda, pinch of salt and baking powder. Whisk into creamed mixture with cocoa mixture.

Spread into two greased and lined 10 inch (25 cm) round cake tins. Bake for about 30 minutes. Cool in tins for 10 minutes.

Meanwhile, melt jam with 3 tbsp (3x15 ml) rum. Remove cakes from tins. Place one on a wire rack, crust side down, and spread with hot jam mixture. Cover with remaining sponge and press together lightly. Cool.

Put chocolate into a heatproof bowl with remaining butter and melt over a pan of simmering water. Remove from heat and beat in sifted icing sugar and rest of rum.

Pour the icing on to the cake and spread quickly with a palette knife. Lift rack and tap it sharply on table so that the icing flows over sides of cake. Allow to set slightly, then mark top into 16 slices. Leave to set.

Flamed fruit salad

Overall timing 30 minutes

Freezing Not suitable

To serve 4

	Selection of any firm fresh fruit: apple, banana, cherries, orange, clementine, pear, peach, straw-berries and grapes	
1	Lemon	1
1 oz	Butter	25 g
3 tbsp	Caster sugar	3x15 ml
2 oz	Flaked almonds	50 g
3 tbsp	Rum	3x15 ml

Prepare the fruit and chop it into pieces. Mix these together in a bowl. Grate lemon and squeeze out juice. Add juice to fruit.

Put the butter and caster sugar into a saucepan. Heat without stirring, until the sugar caramelizes and becomes light brown. This will take about 5 minutes. Add the grated lemon rind and almonds. Cook for about 5 minutes, stirring occasionally, until the caramel and nuts are golden brown.

Remove pan from the heat. Add juices from mixed fruits and stir until caramel becomes a smooth syrup. Add the fruit and heat through for about 5 minutes, turning the mixture over frequently to distribute the syrup. Remove from heat.

Warm rum in a metal ladle, then set it alight and pour over fruit. Serve immediately with whipped cream or ice cream.

Hot apple flan

Overall timing 1 hour

Freezing Not suitable

To serve 6

7 oz	Plain flour	200 g
	Pinch of salt	
1 tbsp	Icing sugar	15 ml
3½ oz	Butter	100 g
Filling		
1½ lb	Cooking apples	700 g
2 oz	Butter	50 g
4½ oz	Icing sugar	140 g
3 tbsp	Calvados or brandy	3x15 ml

Preheat the oven to 400°F (200°C) Gas 6.

To make pastry, sift flour, salt and sugar into a bowl. Add butter and rub in until mixture resembles fine breadcrumbs. Add enough water to mix to a firm dough. Knead lightly. Roll out dough and use to line an 8 inch (20 cm) flan dish. Bake blind for 20–25 minutes.

Meanwhile, make filling. Peel and core apples. Cut into quarters or eighths, depending on size. Melt butter in a saucepan, add apples and cook over a high heat for a few minutes till light brown. Add 4 oz (125 g) icing sugar and 1 tbsp (15 ml) Calvados or brandy. Cover and cook gently till apples are just tender.

Spoon apples and a little of the juice into the warm flan case. Sift over remaining icing sugar. Keep in a warm oven until needed.

Warm remaining Calvados or brandy in a ladle, then pour over apples. Light immediately and take flan to table while still flaming.

Plum soufflé

Overall timing 1 hour

Freezing Not suitable

To serve 6

1½ lb	Ripe plums	700 g
2–4 oz	Sugar	50–125 g
6 tbsp	Water	6x15 ml
2½ oz	Butter	65 g
1 tbsp	Dried breadcrumbs	15 ml
2 oz	Plain flour	50 g
½ pint	Warm milk	300 ml
3	Large eggs	3
	Grated rind of 1 orange	

Preheat oven to 375°F (190°C) Gas 5.

Stone the plums and cut into quarters. Put into a saucepan with the sugar and water. Bring to the boil, cover and simmer for 10 minutes.

Grease a 3 pint (1.7 litre) soufflé dish with ½ oz (15 g) butter and coat with the breadcrumbs. Put two thirds of the plums in the dish with any juice.

Melt the remaining butter in a large saucepan, stir in the flour and cook for 1 minute. Gradually add the warm milk and bring to the boil, stirring constantly. Simmer for 2 minutes, then remove from the heat. Cool slightly.

Separate the eggs. Beat the yolks into the sauce with the orange rind and remaining plums. Whisk the egg whites till stiff but not dry. Stir one spoonful into sauce and fold in remainder. Pour mixture over the plums in the dish.

Stand dish in a roasting tin containing 1 inch (2.5 cm) hot water. Bake for 30–35 minutes till well risen and golden. Serve immediately.

Tipsy fruit pancakes

Overall timing 70 minutes

Freezing Not suitable

To serve 4

4 oz	Plain flour	125 g
2 oz	Caster sugar	50 g
2	Large eggs	2
½ pint	Milk	300 ml
	Pinch of salt	
½ teasp	Vanilla essence	2.5 ml
2 oz	Butter for cooking	50 g
Fruity syrup		
4 oz	Butter	125 g
3½ oz	Sugar	100 g
	Grated rind of ½ lemon	
4 oz	Flaked almonds	125 g
4 tbsp	Orange juice	4x15 ml
3 tbsp	Lemon juice	3x15 ml
6 tbsp	Brandy	6x15 ml
4	Bananas	4

Sift flour and sugar into a mixing bowl. Gradually beat in eggs, milk, salt and essence. Leave to stand for 15 minutes.

Melt a little butter in a 6 inch (15 cm) frying pan. Make eight very thin pancakes. As each is completed, roll it up and keep it warm.

To make fruity syrup, cream butter with sugar and lemon rind. Put into large frying pan. Add almonds and heat for 5 minutes without stirring, till sugar caramelizes. Stir in orange and lemon juices and 2 tbsp (2x15 ml) brandy. Cook for a few minutes more, then add sliced bananas and rolled pancakes. Cook for 3 minutes, spooning syrup over.

Warm remaining brandy in a ladle, pour over pancakes and set alight. Serve flaming.

Baked apricots

Overall timing 1 hour

Freezing Suitable: reheat from frozen in 400°F (200°C) Gas 6 oven for 15 minutes, then add syrup

To serve 6–8

12	Large apricots	12
½ pint	Milk	300 ml
2 tbsp	Custard powder	2x15 ml
1 tbsp	Caster sugar	15 ml
4 oz	Blanched almonds	125 g
5 oz	Macaroons	150 g
1½ oz	Candied orange peel	40 g
	Pinch of ground cinnamon	
6 tbsp	Redcurrant jelly	6x15 ml
4 tbsp	Water	4x15 ml

Preheat the oven to 400°F (200°C) Gas 6.

Halve apricots and remove stones. Arrange, cut sides up, in a greased ovenproof dish.

Prepare the custard according to packet instructions, using the milk, custard powder and sugar. Cool quickly by standing the pan in cold water. Stir the custard frequently to prevent a skin forming.

Chop almonds, macaroons and candied peel finely and stir into the custard with the cinnamon. Fill apricot halves with custard mixture. Bake for 30 minutes.

Meanwhile, mix together the redcurrant jelly and water in a small pan over a low heat. Spoon syrup carefully over the apricots and bake for a further 10 minutes.

Serve hot with whipped cream, or leave to cool, then chill and serve with ice cream or whipped cream.

Pear pie

Overall timing 1 hour 20 minutes plus maceration

Freezing Not suitable

To serve 8

2 lb	Dessert pears	900 g
4 oz	Demerara sugar	125 g
2 tbsp	Lemon juice	2x15 ml
1 lb	Rough puff pastry	450 g
½ pint	Carton of double cream	284 ml
1	Egg	1

Peel and core the pears. Slice thickly into a bowl and add the sugar and lemon juice. Leave to macerate for 2–3 hours.

Preheat the oven to 400°F (200°C) Gas 6. Heat baking tray in the oven.

Roll out two-thirds of the dough on a floured surface and use to line an 8 inch (20 cm) springform tin.

Add half the cream to the pear mixture and mix well. Pile into the flan case. Roll out the remaining dough to a round. Dampen the edges of the dough lining and cover the pears with the dough round. Seal and crimp the edges and decorate the top with leaves made from dough trimmings. Brush the top of the pie with lightly beaten egg.

Place the pie on the baking tray and bake for 25 minutes. Reduce the temperature to 350°F (180°C) Gas 4 and bake for a further 25 minutes, covering the pie lightly with foil if it gets too brown.

Remove the pie from the tin and place on a serving dish. Serve warm with the remaining cream, whipped.

Index

Almond-coated cheesies 8
Alsatian chicken 66
Anchovy ramekins 26
Angel pie 75
Apple:
  Duck with apples and cream 71
  Hot apple flan 91
Apricots, baked 94
Artichokes, fish with 49
Asparagus boats 6
Avocados, Haitiian 35
Spicy avocado mousse 32

Bacon, roast veal with 53
Beef:
  Beef olives 52
  Beef with oranges 50
  Steaks bordelaise 51
Black Forest gâteau 87

Camembert and pickle salad 31
Caraway twists 9
Cassata 77
Cauliflower cheeses, individual 28
Champagne sorbet 78
Cheese:
  Almond-coated cheesies 8
  Camembert and pickle salad 31
  Individual cauliflower cheeses 28
  Pork baked with cheese 59
Chestnut and rice soup 16
Chicken:
  Alsatian chicken 66
  Chicken Kiev 69
  Chicken supreme 68
  Ham and chicken puffs 8
  Normandy chicken soup 17
  Pastry-wrapped stuffed chicken 67
Chicory soup 13
Chilled cucumber and mint soup 20
Chocolate:
  Angel pie 75
  Chocolate kisses 76
  Chocolate rum gâteau 89
  Pears in chocolate sauce 79
Clam chowder 18
Coffee cream dessert 77
Consommé 12
Country-style liver pâté 38
Crab, grapefruit with 30
Crème Chantilly 85
Croquembouche 84
Crown roast of pork 58
Cucumber and mint soup, chilled 20

Duck:
  Duck with apples and cream 71
  Duck with oranges 70

Fish. See also Halibut etc.
Fish with artichokes 49
Fish Bengali 25
Fish goujonettes 22
Fish pudding 29
Fish rolls in whisky sauce 44
Golden fish 49

Flambéed goose 72
Flamed fruit salad 90
French pork spread 37
Fruit. See also Apple, Apricot etc.
  Flamed fruit salad 90
  Tipsy fruit pancakes 93

Gâteaux:
  Black Forest gâteau 87
  Chocolate rum gâteau 89
  Gâteau St Honoré 86
  Praline cream gâteau 88
Ginger sauce, veal escalopes in 56
Golden fish 49
Goose:
  Flambéed goose 72
Grapefruit with crab 30
Grouse:
  Grilled grouse with Marsala
    sauce 73
Guard of honour 62

Haitiian avocados 35
Halibut in tomato sauce 42
Ham and chicken puffs 8
Ham and spinach hors d'oeuvre 24
Herring:
  Grilled herrings with parsley
    butter 45

Kipper toasts 5

Lamb:
  Guard of honour 62
  Lamb cutlets in pastry 65
  Lamb cutlets Villeroi 63
  Pâté-stuffed roast lamb 64
Liver:
  Country-style liver pâté 38
  Liver and mushroom bites 9

Macaroni nests 35
Manhattan clam chowder 18
Marsala sauce, grilled grouse with
  73
Melon on the rocks 83
Monkfish, braised 47
Mousse:
  Spicy avocado mousse 32
Mushroom:
  Fillet of veal with mushroom
    sauce 54
  Mushroom bouchées 7
  Liver and mushroom bites 9
  Stuffed mushrooms 27
Mousse:
  Moules à la marinière 23

Normandy chicken soup 17

Olives, hot stuffed 10
Onion soup with wine 14
Onion tarts 36
Orange:
  Beef with oranges 50
  Duck with oranges 70

Oranges in caramel 80
Oranges Chantilly 76

Pancakes:
  Tipsy fruit pancakes 93
Pastry-wrapped stuffed chicken 67
Pâté:
  Country-style liver pâté 38
  Hot pâté parcels 39
  Pâté-stuffed roast lamb 64
Pear pie 95
Pears in chocolate sauce 79
Plum:
  Braised pork with plum sauce 60
  Plum soufflé 92
Pork:
  Braised pork with plum sauce 60
  Crown roast of pork 58
  French pork spread 37
  Pork baked with cheese 59
  Pork chops in white wine 61
Praline cream gâteau 88
Prawn:
  Haitiian avocados 35
  Prawn cocktail 33
  Prawn soup 15
Prunes, savoury stuffed 11
Pumpkin soup 19

Raspberries jubilee 81
Raspberry charlotte 82

Salami rolls 4
Salmon:
  Baked salmon with herbs 48
Scallop boats 34
Scampi kebabs 46
Smoked salmon mornay 34
Sole niçoise 48
Soufflé:
  Cold strawberry soufflé 74
  Plum soufflé 92
Steaks bordelaise 51
Strawberry:
  Cold strawberry soufflé 74
  Strawberry vacherin 85
Stuffed mushrooms 27
Stuffed olives, hot 10
Sweetbreads Grand Duke 57

Terrine à la maison 40
Terrine, vegetable 41
Tipsy fruit pancakes 93
Trout baked in wine 43

Veal:
  Fillet of veal with mushroom
    sauce 54
  Roast veal with bacon 53
  Veal escalopes in ginger sauce 56
  Wiener schnitzel 55
Vegetable terrine 41

Watercress soup 21
Whisky sauce, fish rolls in 44
Wiener schnitzel 55